BORN

Mike Starkey has provided a powerful aid to help us attain that most desirable and most difficult of goals — seeing clearly what is happening around us.

Dr Anthony Cramp
Emmanuel College, Cambridge

Buy this book. But be warned that its powerful criticisms of consumerism will make you think very hard about what you buy in future.

Tim Cooper
former co-Chair, The Green Party

By the same author
  Frogs and Princes (Poems)

Born to Shop

MIKE STARKEY

MONARCH

EASTBOURNE

Cover design by W James Hammond

The publishers recognise that many
of the brand names depicted on the
cover are registered trademarks.

British Library Cataloguing in Publication Data

Starkey, Michael S., *1963–*
  Born to shop.
  1. Great Britain. Consumer goods. Demand.
  Social aspects. Christian viewpoints
  I. Title
  261.8'5

ISBN 1–85424–066–8 (Monarch)
     0–7324–0432–0 (Albatross)

Co-published in Australia by
Albatross Books, PO Box 320, Sutherland, NSW 2232

Printed in Great Britain for
MONARCH PUBLICATIONS LTD
1 St Anne's Road, Eastbourne, E Sussex BN21 3UN by
Courier International Ltd, Tiptree, Essex
Typeset by Watermark, Hampermill Cottage, Watford WD1 4PL

CONTENTS

FOREWORD

Many of us feel uneasy about the way Western society is going. We live under constant stress with too much to do and not enough time to give to what we know in our hearts are the more important things in life. Perhaps we are also dimly aware that what we see on our TV screens does not quite mesh with the things we find Jesus talking about in the New Testament. It is hard to put our finger on what has gone wrong. It's even harder to know what an alternative way of life would look like in the late twentieth century.

If these are your questions, Mike Starkey's perceptive insights will help you find the answers you have been looking for. He raises the key issues of ordinary everyday life through which we reveal ourselves. It is deeply disturbing, for the consumer culture is not just an external force influencing us from the outside, but an expression of what we want for ourselves and our children.

This book points towards a Christian counter-culture to replace shop counter-culture. It rests not on opting out but on opting in. We must expect to see Christian ideals change not just ourselves, but our generation; not just our families but our whole society. Reading and reflecting on this book will help you join in developing and promoting the new offensive against the material spirit of the age.

Michael Schluter
Cambridge
February 1989

INTRODUCTION

Come On Down!

The crowd is eager and excited, the atmosphere tense. Together they sit, beneath the great lights, waiting. Who would be the Chosen One, the One selected for grace and favour? Every nerve tingles. A voice begins to speak: deep, rich. It summons a name. Everyone gasps. The voice speaks the ritual words the crowd know so well, those words they have heard spoken so often as year follows year: 'COME ON DOWN!!'

The Named One rushes forward, delirious, screaming, laughing, pulling at her hair with excitement. The crowd, feeling her every shade of emotion, cheers, yells. They are shown great treasures and dribble with pleasure as they spy the undreamed-of wealth. Together the Chosen One and crowd celebrate the central mystery of modern life, the profound joy of consumerism.

The Price is Right is not just a popular TV show. It is an embodiment of life in the late twentieth century. It celebrates the dreams and aspirations of a whole generation of Western culture as it opens a gateway to the paradise of unbounded consumer luxury and offers the immortality of fleeting fame before the camera.

Yet as I watched *The Price is Right* something felt very wrong. It seemed ridiculous and degrading to see grown adults caught up in such joy and excitement over a small heap of consumer junk (admittedly, some of it fairly pleasant junk). It was the sort of wild joy I had only ever seen in people's eyes at the moment of religious conversion. Something seemed out of proportion.

But the emotion radiating from the faces of the crowd is not so strange or isolated in the West today. Ask most people what they daydream about and it would be winning the pools, pocketing a fortune from a competition or owning a bigger home, a new kitchen, a new video or CD player. Our most popular and widespread art-form, advertising, proclaims that true contentment is just a credit card away. Consumerism can be seen in the very skylines of our cities – dominated by shopping megastores and commercial tower blocks, our sites of regular pilgrimage. Money and its uses offer the citizens of Western society their meaning in life, purpose, happiness and a sense of personal identity.

If it is true that survival depends upon creatures adapting themselves to their environment, then let me make a prophecy: in the next stage of evolution humans will develop four small, rotating wheels and a wire handle sprouting from their shoulders to guide them along the alleys of shopping malls. They will grow small flaps of skin for the storage of plastic cards and women will grow marsupial-like wire paniers for their children to sit in, their little wheels protruding. That way humans will be best equipped for survival in a consumer age.

Up in the Tree-House

Maybe my unease at watching *The Price is Right* stemmed from memories of childhood. Somehow I had never quite erased the imprint left by tales of misers, princesses, knights and emperors. The message they gave to a small boy in short trousers was that money could not buy happiness. These were tales that said the miser was always in the wrong because he misunderstood the purpose of human life. The greedy were not liberated by their greed but imprisoned. This was rein-forced by a thousand school assembly tales. Like the one about the monkey which put his hand through railings to steal some nuts but found his hand got stuck when he tried to pull it back. He could not have both the stolen nuts and his hand. And the story about the chopsticks in hell and heaven: both places use enormous, six-foot chopsticks to eat, but in hell each person tries to feed himself (and fails), in heaven they feed each other.

Scrooge's conversion came only when he was wrenched out of narrow self-interest and obsession with money bags, when his eyes were forcibly opened and he saw dimensions of life he had not previously known existed. King Midas's folly lay in believing the silly idea that gold can itself become the point of life, rather than just one of its aspects. If characters were wealthy – handsome princes living in palaces, King Solomon, King Arthur – they were praised not for their wealth but their compassion, gallantry, gentleness or wisdom.

Up in the tree-house heroism lay in justice (Robin Hood), valour (Knights of the Round Table), compassion (Beauty and the Beast), a discovery of one's true identity (the Ugly Duckling). Foolishness lay in greed (Scrooge, Hansel and Gretel, Augustus Gloop), pomposity (Toad of Toad Hall, the Emperor's New Clothes), envy (Cinderella's stepmother), or selfish desire for power (the White Witch of Narnia). The stories contained an odd clarity of vision which put avarice, greed and selfishness in their place. They welcomed wealth as a secondary dimension to life, but roared with laughter or wagged a cautionary finger when mammon took on pretensions of greatness, or even claimed to be something which actually mattered very much.

The Real World

But somewhere the moral of the story changed. As you climbed down from the tree-house you realised you were entering a new and unfamiliar landscape. Perhaps you encountered it on the first day at school when you realised the playground was a jungle where only the strong survived. Dreams of valour faded with Father Christmas and the tooth fairies as you understood that in the real world it was the dragons who came out on top and knights were naive idealists who tended to get eaten. Maybe it was on the day you collected your first bike, which you jealously guarded from the covetous eyes of the other kids in your street.

Wherever you might have first encountered the values of the 'real world', they were confirmed in adverts which offered seductive fantasies of possession. They were confirmed as you drifted into town with friends to stare longingly at T-shirts, records and jewellery, scarcely able to bear the emptiness of life without them. They were confirmed in the biology lesson during which you were told that life on earth is essentially about the survival of the fittest and, by implication, that selfishness – far from being a sin – is actually the only universal rule of existence.

They were confirmed by teachers who said most of the early stories you had been told about a loving God were myths invented by a primitive culture with an inadequate understanding of the real world. And by the university lecturer who eloquently explained that not only did God not exist but he wasn't sure if his desk existed either. And the TV expert who said the teachings of Jesus which you had so admired were old-fashioned and restrictive. The values of the 'real world' were contained in the speech by the politician who explained how money had to be created *before* we could indulge in the secondary luxuries of care for nature or provision for the poor and needy.

Into the vacuum left by debunked myths and scorned ideals came consumerism, calling on us to find our identity in purchases, fashions and screen idols. It told us we were truly free if we could choose between a panoply of goodies on megastore shelves. We could find happiness through material things. Greed was the creed; profit, efficiency and pleasure the yardsticks we used to measure what was successful or desirable. The most intense one-minute experience available to modern mankind is that won in a local newspaper quiz where a person is given a minute to rush round a local store in a mad rush of adrenalin and throw all they can into a trolley.

The tale of Scrooge gives us a brief glow of nostalgia for an earlier, slightly dusty morality as we sit in church on Christmas Day or watch the Sunday serial on TV. But then it's back to the real world, in which Scrooges are heroes, Bob Cratchits dispensable, Tiny Tims unproductive spongers off the state.

The Upside-Down World

Then a bizarre realisation. There are people who insist the half-remembered tales of childhood are actually closer to the heart of reality than all the sophistication of the real world. There are those who still cling to the outrageous belief that happiness only comes as we turn real world values on their heads.

The perspective from this upside-down world is one in which consumerism appears as a temporary and ludicrous aberration, in which a veil is lifted and humans are recognised as more than pleasure machines refined from a primeval consommé, not born to shop but to form relationships, seek justice and find their true identity in relation to the Creator. For me, the surprise increased as I realised that many of the great people I admired most shared this vision: C. S. Lewis, G. K. Chesterton, Martin Luther King, Dorothy L. Sayers, Mother Teresa, Desmond Tutu.

For two years I worked as press officer at the Jubilee Centre, a Christian-based political campaigning and research group. The vision behind the Centre was that no area of life could be uncoupled from moral criteria, that economics and politics do not run according to their own laws but must constantly be reassessed with reference to a fixed ethical yardstick. This angered and offended many people, particularly those who believed that the modern creed of consumerism should be allowed to steamroller all other values in its relentless progress, that the wild, uncompromising message of the Bible could be confined to the dustbin of history. This opposition was encountered with force in our campaigns to place a limit on the activities of the credit and lending industry and to oppose the commercialisation of Sunday – the shared day for rest, family and community.

The situation of the consumer West is summarised by the sociologist Tony Campolo in his question, 'Who switched the price tags?'[1] According to Campolo, our society is like a shop which has been broken into. The intruders have stolen nothing, but rearranged all the price tags so the things of great value are marked down as almost worthless, whilst the cheap goods are held to be of enormous worth.

Born to Shop is a kind of romp through the values of the tree-house and those of the commercial 'real' world with the rearranged price tags. It draws examples from a range of specific areas – including advertising, sport, credit, personal identity and the environment. In making comparisons I have tried, quite unashamedly, to challenge some of the cherished assumptions of Western lifestyles and attitudes. At the same time, I have ironically found myself challenging those of the Christians, socialists and 'alternative lifestyle' types who condemn the consumer society out of hand.

The claim of the book is not that greed and selfishness are new problems, peculiar to a consumer age. Quite the reverse. Because people are fallen, imperfect beings they have always been characterised by a liberal dose of greed and selfishness (this side of Eden, at least) and they always will be. The issue at stake is what individuals and nations *do* with this fact. Most cultures, believing in absolute standards of right and wrong, have condemned these qualities as evil or sinful and encouraged people to overcome them. But the West's consumer culture says they are a positive virtue. Traditional morality is reversed, in the name of affluence and progress. The result is a range of problems which really are new and are peculiar to our age and culture. The book takes a look at some of these new problems, including consumer debt, the environmental crisis, the push for commercialising every day of the week and the way in which people root their identity in their consumer purchases.

By way of solutions the book does not point backwards to a supposed Golden Age of either medieval Europe, 'primitive' societies in the developing world or pre-industrial Britain (though I do believe we may have much to learn from these cultures). It certainly does not share the irrational optimism of those who look forward to a day when humans will have evolved into an enlightened super-race. Rather, it roots its hope in the biblical image of a lost Creation in which status, possessions and money counted for nothing. It is in this condition that the real world was first shaped and into this form that it will one day be recreated. The vision of *Born to Shop* is that in our in-between age we can start to experience the reality of the future kingdom and apply its values to every aspect of life, that we can join in a joyful rebellion against the warped ideals of a culture which reduces people to units of consumption and measures their value by the size of their piggy banks. It is a book about modern idolatry.

This is a book of 'what ifs'. What if there really is a great truth to life to which childhood stories pointed? What if the values in the tales actually fitted the real world better than those we have put in their place? What if care for people and nature mattered more than profits? What if the earth really will be inherited by the meek while the affluent sit, eagerly straining to thread their camels through needles? What if it's true that love conquers evil and that greed, far from making you happy, makes you sick?

What if, after all, consumerism has got it wrong?

Notes

1   Tony Campolo, *Who Switched the Price Tags?* (Word: Milton Keynes, 1987).

1

OINKS, WOOPIES AND JOLLIES

The Wonderful World of Advertising

Adverts, Adverts Everywhere...

The modern marketing man no longer stands with a foot in your door giving away lemon squeezers. He has long since packed his case and moved to an air-conditioned office furnished with consumer hardware from which he sells you everything from beans to prime ministers.

It is he, perhaps more than any other person, who determines the environment in which we live, move and have our daydreams. His handiwork forms the backdrop against which we act out our lives.

Advertisements adorn the streets we walk down, the papers and magazines we read, our TV and radio, bus shelters, buses and taxis. Some buses *are* adverts, painted from top to tyre with the colours and logos of products. Adverts surround our sports grounds and colour racing cars, boats, hot-air balloons and sports wear. They are on our supermarket trolleys and fall daily through our letterbox. Schoolchildren sing the songs of the ad-man as they run in the playground, workmen whistle his tunes.

In the words of art critic John Berger, 'No other kind of image confronts us so frequently. In no other form of society in history has there been such a concentration of images, such a density of visual messages.'[1]

In America, home of consumerism, it has been calculated that the average citizen spends more than a year and a half of his or her life just watching TV commercials – around fifty minutes per day. If that sounds unlikely, it has to be pointed out that the average American family watches six-and-a-half hours of television each day.

In the UK the figure is not quite so high. Brits watch six hours in the winter and four-and-a-half in summer and the adverts are not so frequent (a maximum of six minutes per hour, when averaged across total station output, with not more than seven minutes in any given hour). But we too live bombarded by thousands of messages each day, encouraging us to spend, spend, spend. The advert has become a form of universal culture, recognised the world over.

We are even confronted with advertising when we don't realise it. Many of the 'features' in magazines, particularly women's magazines, are little more than rewritten press hand-outs from product manufacturers, designed to focus attention on their product in the guise of an objective look at an issue. Women's magazines are in any case around 60 per cent advertising.

In the cinema, the adverts are not simply brief inserts, preceded by the sound of voices singing, 'pa paa – pa paa – pa paa – pa paa – pa pa paaa'. The advertising can extend into the film itself. James Bond always wears a Seiko watch, Sylvester Stallone has a penchant for Pepsi, Crocodile Dundee snaps up a multitude of cans of Fosters. Many gallons of Coke were planted in *The Killing Fields* – being drunk, blown up and advertised on hoardings.

These were not accidents. They were the results of 'product placement', an alternative form of advertising whereby products appear in films and manufacturers ensure rival brands do not. This form of advertising has the advantages to the advertisers that people don't see it as advertising and that it is associated with people's favourite screen heroes – whom they might go off and emulate.

Something similar has been happening in TV. In 1984 the US channel KCOP-TV was taken to court by the National Assocation for Better Broadcasting. The pressure group was charging that the children's TV programme, *He Man and the Masters of the Universe*, was one long advert for the toys of the same name. In the past toys had commonly followed such shows, to capitalise on their success – toys such as Batman and Superman. But now the very programme was being designed as an advertisement for an already existing toy. Similar accusations have been brought against children's shows on the BBC, such as *Thundercats*.

In the words of Peggy Charren, president of the American group Action for Children's Television, 'If you wanted to make a documentary about Helen Keller (the blind campaigner) in this country, you would have to talk Mattell into doing a Helen Keller doll.'[2]

Adverts colour the music we hear, buy and recognise. At the time I started writing this chapter, the Number One record in the pop charts was an old 60s hit revived by a TV lager advert. When I finished, it was the barely-disguised theme from a Coca-Cola advert. Needless to say, the sleeve of the record has the Coke logo emblazoned across it and the photo on it is not that of the vocalist but two Coke-guzzling teenagers from the TV advert. A large percentage of the records lower down the charts are there due to their use in commercials. Many people go into record shops and ask for 'the Hovis music', unaware of its other connection – with a composer called Dvořák. How many people identify 'I Heard it Through the Grapevine' as the 'half-naked boy in the laundry' song without attributing it to Marvin Gaye? Or the 'Hamlet cigars' tune, without pondering on Bach?

Even those who do not buy a daily paper receive advertising-based papers which often only give a cursory nod in the direction of news, and much of the news and feature material they do use is simply advertising for local companies, masquerading as news. As the TV airwaves open up, along the American model, there will be more and more advertising-based channels.

This chapter is about the inescapable advert. But a word of clarification is needed. A great range of groups advertise, including relief agencies, charities, churches, furniture removers, restaurants and teenagers selling bikes. Specialist magazines – from the religious and sporting press to trade journals such as *Asian Rubbers & Plastics*, *Success Potato* and *Eurofruit* – each have adverts targetted at their own readership. The focus of this book, however, is the single main type of advertising we encounter, that of consumer goods, and all comments will refer to this category of publicity. I have tried to choose examples which are well known, if not always the most recent.

Advertising in the West

Advertising is a product of affluence and mass-production. It barely exists in subsistence cultures, where people work to stay alive. In such cultures workers provide for the immediate needs of their own families and villages and there is not a large amount of surplus luxury goods which need to be sold. Consequently there is no need to stimulate consumption artificially by means of adverts.

Britain has had advertising in a form that we would recognise – newspapers, handbills and posters – since around the seventeenth century. By 1759 Dr Samuel Johnson was commenting that the advertising of his day was 'so near to perfection that it is not easy to propose any improvement.'[3]

The next major step forward for advertising came in the late nineteenth century, as a response to the changing patterns of manufacturing, media and transport. For the first time, mass production meant that many more goods could be produced than were strictly necessary for human survival. This led to attempts to persuade people that although a certain item was not strictly necessary, it would improve their lifestyle to possess it. Information was not enough; a little persuasion had to be used. And the newly developed railway network helped distribute the newly produced, cheap goods.

The idea of the 'brand name' had been around since the early nineteenth century. But with mass production it came into its own. Many products, such as soaps, teas and breads were being produced and each manufacturer needed to give the public a reason to choose his product in preference to his opponent's near-identical one. Brand names, which differentiated similar products, had become common by 1940 – names such as Lipton's, Hovis, Bovril, Pears. It was not long before some brand names became synonymous with the product they identified: you used a Hoover to clean your home, you wrote with a Biro, you stuck paper with Sellotape. Goods had developed a 'personality' of their own and people bought the *brand* they felt they preferred.

It was in the post-war years that consumer advertising took off in a big way. This was the start of modern consumerism as we know it. Large transnational companies, mostly from America, came into their own – Procter and Gamble, Heinz, Nestlé, Kellogg. These were companies who could mass produce foods, cleaning products and consumer goods and they set about creating a mass market.

This proved an easy task. Americans and Europeans were swept along in an economic boom which followed the privations and misery of war. The general mood was one of optimism and hedonism, and the good life was increasingly associated with the possession of more and more of the exciting consumer goods which brought affordable luxury to ordinary working people. Previously such a level of sensual delight had only been available to kings and princes. This applied particularly to the USA, a country rebelling against the puritanism of its first white settlers and its early history of deprivation. Despite the founders' attempts to avoid aristocracy, at last Americans could experience the luxury of royalty and the aristocratic delights of gaining one up on the Joneses. The extravagance was reflected in the large, petrol-guzzling cars of enormous size and with excessive tail-fins and trimmings, the Chevrolets and pink Cadillacs of today's nostalgia. It was the age of gloriously tacky consumer junk, hallmarks of an era celebrated in 'trash' films such as *Hairspray*.

The mood was reflected in the music of the day. Elvis told you not to mess *his* new consumer purchase – his Blue Suede Shoes. Chuck Berry sang the delights of driving the latest model of car. And the records, fashions and trivia of the new stars were themselves cause for more consumer purchases, particularly by the newly-found market – teenagers.

The Media

The changes in manufacturing were accompanied by a shift in the media. By the end of the nineteenth century, newspapers and advertising had become inextricably bound together: the papers provided the audience the advertisers wanted to reach, the advertisers in turn provided the revenue the papers needed to be viable and to keep their cover price affordable.

Commercial radio had been going for over fifty years in the USA by the time it reached the UK in 1973. Commercial television arrived in the US in 1945, in the UK in 1955. Television and advertising embraced at the start of a long-standing love-affair between the two. By 1983 some forty per cent of total money spent on advertising in the UK went on the TV. Television became the new shop window for the luxury goods coming off the assembly lines. As with the press, advertisers and TV needed each other.

The 1950s were the era when advertisers began to experiment with methods of persuasion drawn from psychologists. Advertising boffins such as Ernest Dichter advised companies on how to use the 'depth' approach to advertising, which taught them to reach into and titillate the consumers' unconscious minds, bypassing normal critical faculties. Ad-men realised that by tweaking pangs of guilt, insecurity, lust and ambition, greater results could be obtained than by the simple 'Ho ho ho!' of a Jolly Green Giant. But the underlying message to the consumer never varied: here is how you can attain the good life of prosperity and personal fulfilment.

The Backlash

By the 1970s the mood had begun to change, and again the USA was in the forefront. It was no longer easy to characterise every Westerner as a fun-loving glutton who saw life essentially as a search for new consumer goods, bound to his fellows by a shared definition of the good life. A mood of American disgruntlement following the scandals of the Vietnam War and Watergate was combined with recession and inflation and the resulting belt-tightening in national economies. The 'Woodstock generation' were rebelling against their parents' unthinking materialism and were following the advice of counter-culture guru Timothy Leary to 'drop out'. Many turned to drugs, Eastern religions, Marxism and commune life in a desperate search for the authenticity which they did not see in their parents' consumerism.

Advertising was seen as an embodiment of the hyped, plastic superficiality of materialism. Society was fragmenting into different groups with radically opposing ideals. Many of the new generation were expressing a backlash against consumerism. The advertising industry could see its empire gradually starting to collapse around itself.

Advertising companies, laying off staff in large numbers,

realised they would have to make drastic changes. The pioneer of the new advertising was the US advertising company Young and Rubicam. They consulted not only economists about the future, but also sociologists and psychologists. The result was 'psychographics', a way of targetting the new, diverse groups in society. It treated consumers not just as a fun-loving mass, but rather identified the different groups and worked out strategies for appealing to their respective desires, ambitions, guilts and neuroses.

Psychographics

Many different categories of consumer were identified by psychographics, based on sex, class, hobbies, income and any number of combinations of these factors. Since the early days of psychographics, many others have been identified. But the main system is known as VALS, Values And Life-Styles.

One of the most common versions of VALS divides consumers into five categories:

▷ *Belongers*. These are the traditionalists. They are suspicious of change and like security and familiarity. They are strongly pro-family.

▷ *Emulators*. These are young people, in search of an identity. Unsure of what image to present to the world, they find a self-image from clearly defined groups, role models and heroes.

▷ *Emulator achievers*. These are the yuppies, the pushy, accomplishing types who want to get on in the world and do well for themselves. Factors such as family and community are subordinated to individualistic achievement.

▷ *Societally conscious achievers*. Again, driving and determined, but committed to a quite different ideal. These are the 'alternative' lifestyle types who experiment with new ways of life. They are keen on the environment, social issues and health and reject materialistic values based around consumer goods.

▷ *Need-directed.* These are the very poor. Probably unemployed, and with virtually no disposable income, so almost ignored by advertisers.

Since the introduction of psychographics generally, and VALS in particular, the advertising industry has largely operated on the principle of identifying new target groups and giving them labels. Such groups include DINKS (double income, no kids), OINKS (one income, no kids) and BOBOS (burnt-out but opulent).

Perhaps the biggest discovery has been the growing market amongst the elderly. This has given rise to a plethora of new terms: GRUMPIES (grown-up, mature people), GLAMS (greying, leisured, affluent, middle-aged), WOOPIES (well-off older people), and JOLLIES (jet-setting oldsters with lots of loot). It has also spawned a range of euphemisms for referring to the elderly, including 'September people' and 'grey panthers'. One group, Third Age Research, is paid to quantify the expanding old-age marketplace and tell manufacturers how best to target their advertising.

The Selling of Dreams

With the arrival of psychographics it became possible to present goods to target consumer groups, not simply as a luxury item to enhance their life, but as an extension of themselves. The product becomes an essential part of who they are, or rather, what they *could be*.

For each section of society, adverts operate at the level of daydreams. One of the most famous quotations from the advertising industry is that of Charles Revson, founder of Revlon cosmetics: 'In the laboratory I make cosmetics, in the store I sell dreams.' What is being sold is not a mere product, but an image of yourself – transformed, beautified, more confident, happy; not insecure, unstriking to look at and unfashionable in dress.

For this reason, advertising has to create dissatisfaction and play on people's universal sense of personal inadequacy. The reality of your life is unpleasant, you are told, but with this one purchase it can be transformed. Your job is mundane, you have spots or dandruff, you are surrounded by screaming toddlers, you feel an inner loneliness – but you too could be an odour-free, headache-free, spotless, constantly stimulated piece of seductive humanity. This desire for escape from the mundane aspects of life was recently stated baldly in an advert for Littlewoods Pools. It presented a large, appetising bowl of cherries above the wording, 'It's what life could be'. The media critic Marshall McLuhan describes this function of advertising as 'keeping upset with the Joneses'.[4]

Targetting the Dreams

The images presented to each of the VALS group categories as solutions to the feelings of inadequacy vary from group to group. For Belongers, it is the domestic, super-efficient, caring OXO Mum. It is the scrubbed, eager nuclear family of the breakfast cereal or yoghurt advertisement. It is the advert for Hovis or Mr Kipling's cakes, in which a bumbling old gent speaks of a world where it is always a sunny autumn day, apples grow on gnarled old trees, there is cricket on the village green and cakes are carefully baked individually (rather than by the tens of thousand in a factory).

For young Emulators the image is the Marlboro cowboy, the macho individualist who rides into the sunset in a rough landscape of which he is the master. It is the Coke advert where delirious teenagers dance, play saxophones, balance each other on bike paniers, and run sweating into happy bars at midnight. It is 'that M&Ms feeling', identified as becoming one of the beautiful people with dazzlingly white teeth who laugh their way into a series of clubs and flash cars. It is the Shell advert which shows surf boards, beaches, happy and glamorous people in a customised VW Beetle, and ends with the slogan, 'When you buy Shell, you're buying much more than petrol'. Of course, you aren't, but that is irrelevant. It is an image designed to grab those in need of an appealing, glamorous sense of identity and confidence.

The images for Emulators are particuarly to be seen in cinema advertising, because the 15–24-year-old market is the group which watches least television, but which goes regularly to the cinema.

For the Emulator-Achievers, the image is the dynamic executive who arrives in New York fresh and wily enough to gain the upper hand over his rivals. It is the busy woman whose life is so hectic and packed that she simply has to relax in a Radox bath to allow her successful, tired body to rest. It is the yuppie who swans around his London flat surrounded by the trappings of success, but who still keeps his cockney accent (to advertise butter). It is the American Express advert which tells an individual that when he has reached his stage of life and success he can't manage without the convenience, flexibility and additional prestige brought by an Amex card. According to an American Express direct mail shot, the card is a means for you to 'tell the world – and yourself – you've made it'. It will transport him into a world of opportunities where pretty, uniformed women say, 'Very good, sir.' It is the car advertisement which invites you to see yourself as the driver of a large, powerful motor which others would envy.

This group of Emulator-Achievers is the key market for 'designer' products: overpriced objects for credulous consumers whose desire for exclusivity outweighs their common sense. The debasement of the term 'designer' to imply that only horribly expensive items are designed is a clever piece of nonsense invented to capture the well-moneyed market of status-conscious consumers.

Societally-Conscious Achievers, the fastest-growing group of consumers, are wooed by subtle Perrier water advertisements, which at the same time promote a healthy product and appeal to the viewer's intelligence by their witty puns on 'eau'. They are the target audience for the poster showing a clear mountain scene to advertise lead-free petrol, or the supermarket which advertises in the quality press that none of its aerosols contain damaging chlorofluorocarbons (CFCs) which harm the atmosphere. A new term is coined: 'ozone-friendly'.

Finally the Need-Directed, shunned by most advertisers due to their poverty, become a prime target group for the credit and loan advertisers who frequently advertise in the local and tabloid national press.

Buying Into an Image

In all forms of consumer advertising the image of the product is central. Because one of the main arguments used by advertising's defenders is that adverts provide information, you might expect that the most heavily advertised products would be those we need most information about, such as washing machines, hi-fi or cars. But this is not the case. From the very early days of advertising most creative energy has always been expended in giving an image or personality to things which in themselves have few or no distinguishing characteristics.

One bar of soap may be pretty much the same as another, as may be two rival brands of cigarette or beer. When one product is objectively indistinguishable from the next there is little reason for the consumer to carry on choosing one brand as opposed to its rival. But people can be persuaded to carry on buying a product if they like its image. Brand A soap may not clean you any better than Brand B, but if you feel its image is closer to how you see yourself or how you would like to see yourself, you carry on buying A. Advertising not only gives information about products; by giving image to essentially bland, imageless goods advertising often *is* the product.

You have to drink 'your' lager, the one which most accurately reflects your own personality in some way, although they may all taste virtually indistinguishable. You need to wear 'your' jeans, although they are the same as another pair in every other respect. Or training shoes, washing powder, carbonated water or cigarettes. Children scream if they are given the wrong brand of baked beans. An American friend of mine declaimed at length about the superiority of one brand of quarter pounder hamburger – in the shop where she served – over a rival brand. To her it really mattered. Coke is the *real* thing, although infidels may find it oddly similar to Pepsi or 'own brand' cola, and the Coca-Cola company provides us with a barrage of images to prove us that Coke really is It and nothing else will do.

The author of a recent study of the advertising industry, Eric Clark, illustrates the point with reference to vodka:

> Advertising built vodka into *the* drink of the sixties and seventies, managing to persuade a young public that one brand of an odourless, colourless, tasteless liquid – Smirnoff – was better than other odourless, colourless, tasteless competitors even if it cost more. The higher price – around £1 more a bottle in the UK – was, in fact, part of the process of 'proving' the product was premium and thus superior.'[5]

In many TV and cinema adverts a carefully constructed dream-world of pure image is built up, and it is not until right at the end that you are told what is being advertised. During the advert you sit and ask yourself, 'Is this for lager? Spirits? A bank? British Telecom?' In a way, the product is irrelevant. The key is to portray a scene which fires the imagination and desires and then to imply that the way to achieve the scene is through a shopping trip to buy a product. Many adverts are interchangeable – hot evenings in the Southern States of

America, futuristic worlds where grim, Teutonic men spy through window blinds. It need have no logical relevance at all to the product being advertised.

Twisting the Truth

Under these conditions, traditional notions of 'true' and 'false' become irrelevant. All is pure image. We can ask in vain *how* it is that things should happen after a Badedas bath, *why* 'anything can happen' after Smirnoff, what the relevance of a cowboy is to cigarettes, or spies and bears to lager. Of course, this is missing the point. These are not questions we are accustomed to ask about adverts – we suspend normal categories of 'truth' and 'untruth', as we do in the theatre, and accept a surreal linking of unconnected images in an enticing dreamscape.

This focus on image as opposed to genuine factuality affects the way some manufacturers defend their products, particularly makers of dangerous or unhealthy products. The most common criticism of tobacco is that it kills people. Nicotine gives rise to a variety of medical problems, including lung cancer, heart disease and breathing difficulties. That is a matter of 'true or false': either tobacco kills or it doesn't. We might expect the tobacco industry's Tobacco Advisory Council to offer evidence that it does not. Instead, they shift the ground of argument to freedom of choice. In full page adverts in the national press they launched a broadside at British Airways and local government offices for banning smoking. The advert criticising BA is entitled, 'May a Minority of 17 Million Say a Word?' British Airways are presented as enemies of freedom and the tobacco industry (whom many would identify as the real guilty party) as defenders of liberty.

Similarly, a leaflet by the butter industry, the Facts About Butter, claims with vigour that in the health issue, butter is in fact no more fattening than margarine. That may be true, but it is irrelevant to the main area of contention – butter's high cholesterol content. Most people's reason for switching to margarine is that butter's cholesterol is known to cause problems with blood circulation in the body. But by presenting an *image* of health, other questions – the real questions – are left on one side.

Advertising and its Critics

Because of the way advertising so frequently seems to sidestep issues of truth it has been widely criticised. Malcolm Muggeridge said, with an enthusiastic leap of logic, 'If you are going to advertise it's almost certain that you'll exaggerate, and therefore 90 per cent of advertising is lies.'[6] The Labour politician Aneurin Bevan described advertising as an 'evil service', and Pope John Paul II has said that young people are threatened by 'the evil use of advertising techniques'. Raymond Chandler, the crime novelist, said ads were just 'a waste of talent'. Dorothy L. Sayers, another crime writer who worked for several years in an advertising agency, has written:

> A society in which consumption has to be artificially stimulated in order to keep production going is a society founded upon trash and waste, and such a society is a house built on sand.'[7]

In 1957 the American author Vance Packard shocked the West with his book *The Hidden Persuaders*, an exposé of the advertising of his day. It portrayed an increasingly Orwellian world where Big Brother manipulated us through advertising which sank into our unconscious and made us act against our rational will. And, on an even more melodramatic note, Professor Wilson Brian Key's *Subliminal Seduction* (1974) saw sexual and other innuendo hidden in virtually every advert. This included finding the letters S-E-X hidden in one ad, just beyond the grasp of the rational mind, in some ice cubes.

The argument of many of these critics is that advertising

deprives people of freedom to choose in a detached, logical way which balances facts. From some, the call has gone out to ban advertising completely because of its pernicious effects, or at least to introduce very severe restrictions. But this position has problems:

▷ There are already a vast array of restrictions on advertising, including more than fifty Acts of Parliament. There can be no political, religious, tobacco or charity advertising on TV. There are limits on what medicines and financial services can be publicised, as well as how drink can be presented. TV companies can veto ads they deem unsuitable, and there are industry guidelines relating to taste and decency.

▷ Adverts are a bright, fun, witty aspect of life. Our streets and TV screens would be duller without them.

▷ Without advertising to support them most of the media, much sport and some areas of the arts would simply collapse overnight. As somebody who has worked in commercial radio and advertising-funded magazines, that's not a prospect I relish!

▷ Because adverts are simply the embodiment of a wider attitude to life in our society, their removal would in itself not remove the underlying values which produced a society of advertising images.

Nonetheless, some tightening up of existing laws could take place. I would personally like to see the ban on advertising cigarettes on TV extended to all tobacco advertising of any kind. The moral overtones of encouraging somebody to become addicted to something which may well kill them prematurely are serious. The media reliance on tobacco advertising revenue inhibits them from dealing in a balanced way with tobacco as a health issue. If a publication says anything damning about the weed, revenue is likely to be withdrawn.

Another form of adverts I believe should be banned entirely are adverts for illegal activities. One example of this is adverts which publicise the illegal opening of, say, a DIY store on Sunday (this happened frequently at the time of the 1986 Shops Bill on Sunday trading). Encouraging people to break the law is also a serious matter.

Another area where the law could be tightened up is in credit and loan advertising. This is an area discussed further in the chapter on debt, but suffice to say here that many people are ending up in debt because they do not fully understand from adverts for financial services just what they are letting themselves in for. This is an area where greater clarity, explanation and even 'health warnings' are needed.

Reassessing Our Attitudes

The main area where action is needed is our own attitudes. Rather than being passive, unquestioning recipients of ads we need to look at them critically, to decode them by approaching them with the eyes of a private detective, trying to cut through layers of alibis, half-truth and image to get at the facts beneath. Advertising forms a significant part of modern culture. It is one of the forms of human communication we encounter most often, every day of our lives, and we need to understand how to approach it, just as we need to learn money management, literacy and healthy eating habits. In our sceptical age, where we are taught to look with caution at all religions, philosophies and '-isms', it seems odd that we allow ourselves – and our children – to soak up the subtle messages of adverts so uncritically.

Analysis of advertising could fit neatly into the school curriculum, from primary school upwards. In secondary education it could take place in Personal Development lessons, Economics, General Studies or even Religious Studies (since ads embody a whole world-view and philosophy, as we shall see). Nottinghamshire Education Authority has produced a Consumer Education Pack for schools (available on request), which contains materials on understanding advertising, and it is a move which other areas might do well to follow.

Advertising: Symbol of the Free World

The main response from the advertising industry to its critics is that it stands for freedom of choice. Not for us the grey uniformity of advertising-free Eastern Europe or the lack of choice of a Soviet grocery. Our exciting diversity is celebrated by advertising as it promotes a huge range of goods and several manufacturers compete in a marketplace with a diversity of goods. A consumer paradise!

It is not a great step of logic to say that advertising is therefore a symbol of the free world itself. Advertising equals freedom in the battle against totalitarianism and oppression. Advertising equals human rights.

However, this argument has two major flaws. It is true that advertising is a part of the landscape of the democratic West. But it is wrong to say that in itself advertising represents genuine freedom of choice, even in goods. As we have already noticed, advertising is used most often to give a spurious 'personality' to essentially identical goods. Where is the freedom to choose between 30 identical cigarettes, lagers, pairs of jeans or floor cleaners? And many of the stores which offer a genuine alternative to the countless hosts of mass-produced items don't advertise. The Body Shop chain, with its focus on high-quality, cruelty-free and environmentally safe goods, is an obvious example.

The second, and more important, flaw in the 'ads/freedom' equation is that freedom to choose between consumer products is only one sort of freedom, and in fact probably one of its least important forms. It completely ignores – in fact denies – the freedom to opt out of the consumer system, to choose a way of life which is not overshadowed by the need to acquire goods and prove one's worth through purchases.

The 'freedom' argument assumes that because the messages of adverts are different – different products are promoted, using different images and different personalities – our ability to choose between many options is enhanced. But though messages of individual ads may differ, the message of consumer advertising taken as a whole is always the same. It is that personal fulfilment, happiness, meaning and identity can come through buying goods.

Icons of Western Life

The true potency of adverts is not so much, as some critics have warned, in the seductive and subliminal messages of particular ads. This is borne out by the fact that 80 per cent of all new food products launched in the UK – most of them backed by advertising – fail to take off. Rather, the power of advertising lies in the message which comes across from all adverts. As such, all consumer adverts are *icons* of Western consumer society. An icon is a form of art which embodies something of the dreams and ideals of the age and the artist which produced it. In medieval Europe icons of the Virgin and Child inspired the faithful to devotion, meditation and prayer. The icons were a statement about the shared faith of the age.

Likewise, 'primitive' cultures produce their own icons – masks, wall paintings, totem poles – which embody a shared faith. An icon is a way of interpreting reality, of understanding the world around you. An icon helps to give meaning to life.

The advert is the icon of our culture. Or, in the words of the media critic Raymond Williams, advertising is 'the official art of modern capitalist society'. It is society having its day-dreams, it is its romantic art. It reflects, glamourises and justifies its basic ideals. In this sense, advertising is for the West what the propagandistic wall-poster is for the Eastern bloc.

The message of our icons is that consumption is the answer to a range of basic human questions. What is the point of life? It is to make money, live in a comfortable house and experience the 'good life' provided by the time-saving devices and luxury goods shown in the ads. What is happiness? You will be happy if you can get your hands on *this* product. What is freedom? It is the ability to choose between the maximum number of consumer goods. What is success? It is having a better car, a better equipped kitchen, a higher income, smarter clothes than the next person.

But the icons have the result of identifying human achievement and aspiration with a narrow range of goals. It leaves no basis for questioning the very presuppositions of the system. This is true both in terms of human values and also in a spiritual sense. First, values.

The values of consumerism are those of individualism, personal fulfilment and material prosperity. My human energies are to be channelled towards attaining a higher standard of living for myself and looking after my own needs and desires. At the economic level, the outlook is justified by the notion that as each person pursues their own prosperity, the total happiness of society as a whole will rise. The icons know nothing of fulfilment through channelling my energies towards others' needs, care for the environment, fostering deep human relationships or working for relief of suffering or poverty. Consumer advertising channels all our desires for a better world towards a striving for consumer goods and personal prosperity.

Real issues such as freedom not to be poor or suffer injustice or to have an unpolluted earth, or not to be in debt, or to have one day set aside for rest and relationships, are just not on the agenda. We are not given the information on which to base truly informed choices. In the words of journalist Jeremy Seabrook:

> If we do not know who has suffered in the production of the most trivial comodities, how can we judge what our choices mean? And if we cannot – or will not – judge, how can they be free choices at all?"[8]

'What is the matter? You have all these goods to choose from!' replies consumerism, unable to see why we are still restless and angry, and why we still feel unsatisfied, even after we have bought each longed-for product. Consumer 'freedom of choice' actually benefits the system more than its individual consumers, glossing over our desire to see social transformation with illusions based on one, narrow definition of personal freedom.

The language of advertising is well analysed by Lewis Blackwell, editor of *Creative Review*, a magazine read by the advertising industry. He is referring to the state of advertising at the particular time he was writing his editorial, but he could equally be describing the iconic language of all adverts:

> Lust and greed have their uses, but the language of international creativity must ensure it has a wider vocabulary. For commercial communication is in the forefront of creating new cultures, and it would be nice if our new societies aspired to more than rape, pillage and affairs with cars and chocolate bars.'[9]

As icons, adverts touch on deeper questions – issues of life and spirituality. They embody not only human values but also religious ideals. A person's religion is his or her framework for understanding life and the world, their world-view. It then explains the point of living and gives a reason to live to tomorrow. It helps you identify which aspects of experience are actually significant and of lasting value. A religion gives meaning.

Consumerism has its answers for all these questions and more. It purports to identify the problem of the world – you are unfulfilled, restless, not reaching your full potential. It offers salvation – buy this product and you will not feel lonely, you will feel good about yourself, you will be a more attractive person. You need not accept the current unsatisfactory situation, it tells you, for you can be born again into a new, transformed person by means of this item. You can be redeemed.

The forerunner of advertising is religion. More than that,

the icons of advertising offer us a new brand of salvation. Consumer icons channel spiritual quest towards a new birth in a consumer paradise of sensual experience, glamour and personal success. It provides its answers for all the questions which have pushed people to seek for God. And it sneers at solutions which proclaim that mammon is to be dethroned.

In the same way that consumer icons treat all human values other than self-fulfilment as irrelevant, so consumerism ignores all claims to find deeper truth and purpose by any means other than the purely commercial. It tells you that 'Coke is It' and 'I think therefore IBM', discouraging a study of how earlier civilizations have found a very different brand of salvation. Become a Johnson's Baby! Live in Marlboro Country! Wear your Ring of Confidence! ...And everything will be OK. Consumerism likes to think it has all the answers.

Notes

1 John Berger, *Ways of Seeing* (Penguin Books: London, 1972) p 129.
2 Quoted in 'US Cuts TV Adverts Aimed at Children', *The Guardian* 10 June 1988.
3 Quoted in John Sinclair, *Images Incorporated* (Croom Helm: Beckenham, 1987) p 6.
4 Marshall McLuhan, *Understanding Media* (Ark: London, 1987) p 226.
5 Eric Clark, *The Want Makers* (Hodder & Stoughton: London, 1988) p 260.
6 Malcolm Muggeridge, *Muggeridge Through the Microphone* (BBC: London, 1967) p 33.
7 Dorothy L. Sayers, *Creed or Chaos* (Methuen: London, 1947) p 470.
8 Jeremy Seabrook, 'Stereotypes in Advertising', *New Society* 18 March 1988.
9 Lewis Blackwell, Editorial, *Creative Review* July 1988.

2

I SHOP THEREFORE I AM

Consumerism and Human Identity

The Identity Vacuum

One of the latest toys for the business executive is the artificial car-phone. The box housing the hollow plastic object boasts that you too can boost your image and status, for a mere £3.99.

Each of us has a sense of identity, a way of making sense of who we are and how we relate to other people and the world around us. The artificial car-phone is a mark of a society in which people root their sense of identity in status and personal possessions. If advertisers categorise us in terms of our consumption and try to channel our yearnings towards material ends, we have made their dream come true by accepting these definitions. My identity is rooted in my purchases. I shop therefore I am.

But this has not always been the case. Shopping has simply filled a vacuum. It is the late twentieth century filling to a hole dug by the gradual removal of all other means that people have traditionally used for gaining a sense of identity. It is our solution to an identity crisis.

Roots of Identity

It is worth looking briefly at the ways people have traditionally found a sense of roots and how the modern age has dug up
each of the roots in turn. The main categories are family,
faith, values, vocation and community.

Family

Traditional cultures have always held the family unit to be the
basic unit of society. The same was true in pre- industrial Britain too. This has generally been the extended family, of
grandparents, aunts, nieces, Old Uncle Tom Cobbley and all.
A sense of belonging to a clan, with its own rituals, habits and
customs – and dress, such as a tartan – was fundamental to
how a person saw him or herself. When people worked on the
land this land was often family-owned. Households were large
and family roles clearly defined. Family was inseparable from
making a living: all the workers were your relatives.

But the Western family has been shrinking, from wider
family to nuclear family (two parents plus a handful of children) to the situation today where only one household in five
is a conventional nuclear family. And the nuclear families
which have survived are besieged by pressures. The small
unit, no longer supported by the wider family, is vulnerable.
One marriage in three ends in divorce – one in two in some
parts of the West.

Additional stress is created by the pressures of much modern work. This tension between job and family was assumed
by a series of advertisements for British Telecom time-saving
devices. The ads asked the executive, 'Would your life be
easier if you'd married the boss?' and 'If your five-year-old
son were asked to draw a picture of his family would you be in
it?'

Once people saw the family as central, with a right to place demands and obligations on family members. Now this has been reversed and we are more likely to see a partner as a way of meeting *my* emotional, sexual and other needs. And if they fail to do so I can opt out. A notion of mutual submission in marriage, such as that of the New Testament, is perceived as oppressive to personal development. The family is no longer the fixed point from which I gain my bearings, and which imposes duties and obligations on me (such as to elderly relatives) and which tells me who I am. It is one of the items of baggage I carry with me as I make my own way through life, useful as long as it brings me happiness.

Faith

All through history mankind has thought itself to be essentially different from animals, vegetables and stones. In a Christian framework this is because mankind is made in the image of God. The creature's identity is inextricably bound up in the identity of the Creator. The parameters for life are set by the guidelines given by him, as are our goals and means.

For centuries Bunyan's pilgrim acted as a role model for identity in Britain, as had the saints of Catholic Europe. Life was a gradual discovery of the will of God.

But in a largely post-Christian age this source of self-discovery has been severed. Religious belief is 'irrational', 'unscientific' or 'old-fashioned'. According to the publicity of one major missionary organisation, there are more Avon Ladies selling cosmetics in the USA than there are full-time missionaries in the whole world. Not surprisingly, much of the Islamic opposition to the Western way of life is over the atheistic consumerism so many of us unquestioningly espouse. Some modern Christian theologians have helped the process along by collapsing the faith from within. In the name of relevance or rationality they have ditched anything which smacks of the supernatural, often ending up with an odd Santa Claus in the sky who prefers to keep himself to himself. The result, in the words of sociologist Peter Berger, has been a

sense of 'homelessness in the cosmos'. Man is a speck on a
lump of rock in a corner of the universe. He feels tiny, insig-
nificant and uncertain of his identity. He no longer relates 'upwards' to a higher power, but downwards to the earth. Mankind is not essentially different from the animals, there is no
objective moral law given from outside which you need to
conform yourself to. You're on your own, buddy.

Values

Even people not confessing the Christian faith, or any other
religion, have tried to keep to some sort of moral principles or
values. The values you hold say something about the kind of
person you are. But in the last couple of centuries, values have
been under attack, from thinkers such as Marx and Freud.

According to Marx, capitalist states exist simply to serve
the interests of the ruling class. They control society in their
interest, concentrate wealth and influence in their hands.
Since resources are limited, the police, legal system and
courts are designed to keep the privileges for the few. From
Marx's perspective, our cherished values about law and order
and good government are simply a smoke-screen to mask our
self-interest.

Freud said we might uphold good, middle-class morality in
public, but below the surface we are each a mass of sexual
energy, libido, which could break out and shatter all our
polite taboos. We could all commit unspeakable acts if we
weren't so careful to repress our true feelings. So society is
built on repression, our neuroses spring from pushing down
our natural instincts. Our values are just a front for the lusts
which we mask and occasionally emerge in 'Freudian slips'.
Our stated values are at odds with the reality of things.

Added to this is the fact that in a modern scientific age we
trust in things which can be 'proved' or measured. Odd,
abstract ideas such as values are subjective and harder to cope
with and make definite statements about. So as God slips out
through the back door, we throw the notion of solid, universal

morals after him. But if there is no universal, objective morality, rooted in the character of God, how should I behave?
What guidelines should I use?

Vocation

In medieval society, each person knew their role in life. Like
a great pack of Happy Families cards, a person's identity was
bound up in their job: Mrs Robinson the ham-smoker, Master
Jones the baker, Miss Johnson the washer-woman. And frequently surnames reflected function; so, to take a few
examples from the current Tory front bench: Thatcher,
Baker, Clarke are all names which would once have designated a profession. But times have changed.

Career is widely seen as a means to acquire wealth, move up
in the world and gain personal status. A job is the vehicle
which transports you to a higher standard of consumption.

Since the Industrial Revolution many jobs have involved
working on production lines, and are characterised by tedium
and lack of personal involvement. Work is something to be
escaped, rather than an extention of yourself. Your leisure
time is when the 'real you' can surface.

And yet we continue to try to root identities in jobs, even if
they are bland and unfulfilling. It is questionable if we should
have the 'work ethic' which sees paid work as an extension of
identity, but by and large we do. So the problem of identity
can be acute for those without paid jobs. If you can't say 'I am
a dock worker/journalist/nurse', and so on, then the obvious
question is 'Who and what am I?'

The opposite extreme faces some college leavers: over-
choice. Faced with a bewildering range of options, how am I
to decide what to do? How can I possibly select just one?
What sort of person am I? Often the answer returns, 'I've no
idea'.

Community

In pre-industrial Britain and in most developing countries a key sense of belonging came from the close relationships in the community in which you lived. Everybody knew everybody, people only used back doors and lived in each other's kitchens. Often the whole community would have a shared profession: fishing, mining, agriculture. You worked, drank, worshipped, played and philosophised with the same, relatively small group of people. In Jersey whole communities would get together to make the annual 'black butter' of cider and liquorice. Some would play music, others danced whilst some made the butter.

Today the ethic has shifted from community to mobility, the 'On your bike!' philosophy where we follow the Pied Piper of job promotion. In our suburban semis, where we see our neighbours once a month as we clean the car, most of us no longer feel the pull of community. Our identity is rooted in smaller units, hidden by net curtains.

If we are amputees, suffering the loss of family, faith, values, vocation and community as earth in which to root our identity, what is left? The answer is me and my need for personal fulfilment. The line from John Donne's famous poem no longer rings true: most men and women today *are* islands, desperately looking for who they are, craving identity, victims of an age which implicitly writes off as puritanical, irrelevant or outdated most of the ways in which humans down the centuries have found that very identity.

At the level of the street and subway the ache for identity is scrawled in aerosol letters, an attempt to assert personality in an anonymous world. It is the writing on the wall for a society which removes from teenagers a solid basis for identity, morality and heroism. Graffitti can be a cry for identity.

Mindless? Antisocial? Maybe. But graffitti and vandalism are only the street equivalent of an alienation felt at every level of society, from the glue-sniffing adolescent to the Oxbridge tutor and playwright. It is the same sense of the loss of meaning expressed no less violently in Beckett's play *Wait-*

ing For Godot, the sculptures of Giacommetti, the modern art of Dada and Surrealism and beyond, and modern linguistic philosophy.

Consumerising Identity

Enter the advertisers. From offices in the West End of London and New York's Madison Avenue they strive to channel our crisis of identity towards consumption. They present images for us to buy into, off-the-peg identities which demand no more from us than a flick of the Visa card. You are what you buy.

You might expect there to be an outcry against the marketing of identities. The reason there is not is because we are happy to accept the images. In the absence of other solid sources of identity, we are glad to root it in our purchases. So today making and spending money are more important than in the past. They are an expression of who we are. A survey by the advertising agency McCann Erickson showed that when asked what makes for happiness, British teenagers put money above friends and love. The report stated (or perhaps *understated*): 'Choice has become increasingly important and consumption is one route towards establishing identity and individuality.'[1]

A director of the agency, Christine Bestell, said of the teenagers surveyed:

> They have short-term goals and many are practical and materialistic. The overriding discovery was the feeling that money was the doorway to modern life and that to consume is to have worth.[2]

As teenagers grow into adulthood, the initiation rites to being seen as grown-up have an oddly consumerist ring to them: owning your own bike, drinking beer, smoking, a stereo, a car, a house. Our age has been described as the 'I want it now generation' and 'the Me-Generation'. In the West money is sexier than sex.

This can certainly be seen in the popular novels at station bookstalls from a new generation of novelists. Sex is old hat. The compulsory erotica pall next to the rampant scenes of passionately making money.

The jackets of a few recent popular novels promised the reader a journey into staggering affluence and glamour:

> They are the glamorous, wealthy women who call the shots behind the closed doors of America's capital. (*Washington Wives*)

> Olivia Steele has everything going for her when she joins the prestigious merchant bank.... From high finance in London to the jet-setting lifestyles of the expatriate rich in Italy and Greece... (*The Indiscretion*)

> The first lady governor of New Mexico – powerful, ambitious, wealthy... A gripping novel of rags to riches. (*Distinctions of Class*)

> From London to Las Vegas, Hollywood to Athens... in the most sophisticated hotels and fashionable nightspots... a jet-set lifestyle of love between black satin sheets and diamonds with very dangerous connections. (*The Bitch*)

In the words of journalist Jeremy Seabrook, writing in *New Society*: 'The instant of buying is the most intense and concentrated experience that our culture offers to the individual.'[3]

The mood has found its way into our films, which increasingly present an exploration of affluent yuppiedom. Oliver Stone's *Wall Street* offers the character Gordon Gekko, acted by Michael Douglas, an entrepreneur characterised by such quotes as 'lunch is for wimps', selling a building was 'better than sex', and saying that greed is 'the essence of the evolutionary spirit'.

Stone created Gekko deliberately to offend the materialistic youth of America and to shock them by parody and over-statement. But when the film hit the American screens many of the audience stood up during Gekko's most passionate hymn to avarice, and cheered.

In early 1988 the British comedian Harry Enfield created the character of an obnoxious cockney, 'Loadsamoney', obsessed with 'dosh'. As a left-wing politics graduate, Enfield intended to satirise what he saw as the uncaring mammon-worship of Thatcherite Britain. But soon real people adopted the phrase, 'Loadsamoney' with relish. Stone and Enfield seem to have been so much in tune with the mood of their day that their irony was missed by many people.

The 'Loadsamoney' mentality has influenced our attitude to our leisure time: we spend money on endless equipment to enjoy our little leisure time to the full. When Britons go on holiday, their two favourite activities, according to official surveys, are shopping and watching TV.

The Me-Generation

The 'Me-Generation' is the product of post-war affluence. It is the generation born in the baby-boom of the 1940–60s, raised in a time of unparallelled plenty. Teenagers, in particu-lar, had money and independence for the first time. Actors such as James Dean appeared on the screens, embodying the awkward 1950s teenager who rebelled against his parents' empty values and who found identity in motor-bikes, leather jackets, soft drinks and rock'n'roll records.

A new market for the advertisers was born, the age group most acutely in search of an identity. A new mass of products was suddenly aimed at providing that sense of identity. By the second half of the 1960s, nearly half of all clothing in the West (with the one exception of underwear) was being bought by the 15–19 year-old market. Banks too started appealing to teenagers to woo the newly found disposable income.

The heroes of the new age were less those whose actions or values you admired but those whose *image* you desired to associate with: James Dean, Marilyn Monroe, Elvis, Jack Kerouac.

An entire generation was brought up surrounded by encouragement to associate identity with image and image with buying certain products. The encouragements came not only from advertisers but from the example of parents, who were enjoying to the full the years of 'You've never had it so good'.

And, although hippies and student radicals shouted against the evils of capitalism, few wanted a return to what they saw as Victorian institutions such as the family, church and a tight code of morality as a basis for identity. Their call was for personal freedom, self-fulfilment and an absence of the restraining hand of oppressive authorities – in fact, the same values shared by the merry consumers of the day, those they were supposed to be rebelling against. The would-be rebels simply bought cocaine instead of Coca-Cola, love-beads instead of lipstick, Marx and the Maharishi instead of Mills and Boon, Dylan instead of Dion and the Belmonts.

Buying an Image

And here we are, so used to associating identity with image that we no longer notice we are doing it. We walk up and down the High Street with the bag which best expresses our image: Fortnum and Mason, Next, Top Shop, Laura Ashley, Body Shop, Oxfam. We wear original Levi 501s to show we are the sort of people who insist on the very best rather than a cheap imitation. We wear clothes with the label on the outside to show the kind of style we have bought into. One shopkeeper recently complained that people came into his store and cut off the small green crocodile logos to stick onto their own clothing, leaving gaping holes in those on sale.

We drive a big car to show we are big businessmen, a 2CV to show we're off to Greenham Common, a sports car to show we're young, footloose and very available. We drive a Morgan to show we're affluent individualists, a Rolls-Royce to tell people we're just plain affluent, a Volvo to show people we go for quality rather than frivolity. And writers of books on consumerism go for a reliable but stylish VW Golf – bright red, to give a hint of fun, and witty rear-window stickers to show they have a sophisticated sense of humour.

We smoke in the first place to show we're a bit of a rebel, grown up, we have style. We smoke Marlboro or Camel because we're the rugged outdoor type, Rothmans because we're smooth and self-assured, Virginia Slims because we're dynamic young American women.

We drink Martini because we're sophisticated, old whisky because we're debonair and discerning, Perrier because we're health freaks, Pepsi because we're pretty cool teenage dudes, imported lager because we're cosmopolitan yuppies, cheap draught lager because oi'm one of der lads and you'd better not mess wiv me. During 1988 no fewer than ninety-two beers and lagers were advertised on British TV.

And so on with perfumes, shampoos, furniture, hi-fi and food. The extent to which we are buying into the image and not for any inherent property of the item is seen when a product remains the same but the image used to sell it changes. This is nowhere clearer than in our image of what constitutes masculine and feminine.

Sex and Image

Take the modern image of masculinity. What might some of the elements be? After-shave, pint of lager, Marlboro cigarette hanging carelessly from the :nouth? Twenty-five years ago everybody thought it was unmanly for a male to wear perfume or fragrances of any kind. Then they called a product after-shave and splashed adverts for it all over, in which it was associated with rugged men, fingered by lustful women driven wild by the smell. So now we wear after shave in the belief that it enhances our masculinity.

Marlboro cigarettes were launched as the lady's cigarette and continued to be seen that way until the cowboys, horses and arid, rocky landscapes arrived on the scene. Lager used to be the lady's drink, to be sipped slowly and with decorum. The concept of today's 'lager lout' would have been meaningless; real men drank bitter. Then lager began to be advertised with images of rugged Australian landscapes and rugged Australians, and rugby teams. Suddenly lager was macho and men, keen to prove they were too, bought into the image.

Our picture of what is feminine is shaped by the images we are shown: for many women it is the dark-eyed waif with large, pouting lips and flat chest, from the fashion catalogue. That is the standard of beauty to which all aspire. The clothes, toiletries and hairstyles we buy – and the mannerisms we adopt – all help to move us away from the ugly reality about ourselves to the sublime ideal on the printed page. For some the ideal is the zeppelin-breasted, painted dolly bird of the girlie magazine. For the eighteenth century and earlier centuries in Europe it was the plump woman with lardy thighs and wobbling stomach.

Our concept of the relative roles of men and women are also to a large extent shaped by the images we see in the media. American studies from the 1970s contrasted the presence of the sexes in TV adverts. The results were quite an eye-opener:

▷ For every ad featuring only women there were three featuring only men.

▷ Of all the ads analysed, only six per cent used a female voice-over. A male voice was used on 87 per cent. The remainder used one male and one female.

▷ Of all ads using females, 75 per cent were for kitchen or bathroom products.

▷ Of the females in the ads, 38 per cent were situated in the home, compared to only 14 per cent of the males.

▷ Twice as many women as men were shown with children.[4]

The commercials showed women being 'marginalised'. They were seen and heard less often than men, so being female was abnormal in the world conjured up in TV adverts. Women were silent and passive, men active and visible. And women were marginalised in that the world of paid work was presented as a male preserve. Woman equalled children, kitchen and bathroom. The adverts were doubtless reflecting a wider attitude to gender roles in 1970s America, but it is like the chicken and the egg. Perhaps one of the main reasons we have such stereotypes is because we see them reinforced so often in commercials.

We find and express identity in the papers and magazines we buy: are you a *Cosmo* woman, or do you buy *Woman's Own*, *Options* or *Over 21*, *Woman* or *Bella*? Or *Spare Rib*? Are you a clergyman who buys the *Church Times* or the *Church of England Newspaper*? Are you the *Guardian* type or the *Telegraph*, the *Sun* or the *Mirror*? Each has a definite image associated with it. An image where we can root a sense of identity.

Consumer Relationships

We even express much of the content of our relationships in consumer terms. We prove we care by buying goods for the loved one. In this we we can justify buying what would otherwise be considered unnecessary luxuries if the item was for ourselves. It is to show the depth of your love or friendship. In a fascinating book, *All You Love is Need*, the sociologist Tony Walter underlines the way we use love to excuse many of the excesses of consumerism: 'So it is that family members see their own purchases as motivated by need and love, but when they look at other households from the outside they see only greed.'[5]

When, in late 1988, the Labour leader Neil Kinnock attacked Mrs Thatcher for encouraging an attitude of greed, her response was to ask whether the desire to do the best by one's loved ones was greed. Sadly, the answer has to be yes – it can be. In a consumer society where care is expressed in cash terms, compassion and greedy consumerism can be the same thing, when measured against objective standards. But you don't see it as greed, you see it as care.

This can have serious consequences at times such as Christmas. A poor family who can afford few presents feels they are unable to express love to the children adequately. If you can't buy the latest gimmick which other parents are buying, you seem to be a less caring parent in a society where 'I love you' often has a price tag.

And for people at any level of society, giving expensive gifts can be a substitute for giving time and affection and giving of yourself. It has become something of a movie cliché to see the wealthy husband who is so caught up in his business affairs that he neglects his wife, and is surprised when she rejects his costly gifts. The hackneyed Hollywood drama of the situation should not blind us to its reality in the lives of many in the modern world. When we are no longer able to give of ourselves we can still give presents. Let us check ourselves, that (as we say during a church offertory) our gifts are simply an aspect or symbol of our self-giving, not a substitute for it.

Fashion and Identity

Perhaps the main way we express our identity in a consumer society is by what we wear. In earlier centuries only royalty and nobility could afford fashion as we know it, and it was only in the post-Second-World-War ‧West that mass-produced, ready-to-wear clothing became an option for everybody.

Not only did people have money in their pockets to buy the fashions, there was a social reason why people took to the exciting new clothing with such enthusiasm. Life in the modern city is anonymous. Today's city-dweller probably sees more people in a single week than a medieval person did in a whole lifetime. We are packed into underground trains with hundreds of people we don't know and will probably never see again; we push past hundreds more as we walk down busy shopping streets. It is a reversal of the medieval world in which a person formed a few, very close relationships in the family and community. City life involves thousands of absolutely superficial relationships – at the level of a glance.

It is impossible to communicate anything of yourself verbally to all these people, but it can be done by images. In a world where fashion is accessible and relatively cheap, everybody can experience the creativity of the artist or writer. You can make yourself a work of art, an aesthetic object which communicates you to the outside world. According to the fashion writer Elizabeth Wilson, fashion is a 'poster for one's act'.[6]

The West is becoming increasingly familiar with the (originally American) 'dress for success' creed. According to one dress for success speaker, 'Sixty-five per cent of someone's evaluation of you is based on your clothing. Clothes are the tool to get what you want.'[7]

A friend once told me she could never agree to go out with a boy after meeting him in a swimming pool or the sea. 'After all,' she reasoned, 'he might be the type who wears flares.' Clothing is inseparable from identity. In a society which is losing its grasp on heroism in terms of faith and values, the street heroism each one of us can indulge in is fashion. Our appearance can startle, stun, excite, cause admiration and emulation.

Established companies such as Marks & Spencer, Next and Laura Ashley create a whole lifestyle wardrobe of co-ordinated shapes and colours for every moment of a woman's life.

It is a complete package which you can buy into. The same is true of shops for teenagers and, increasingly, men too.

Counter-cultures also express their identity primarily in their clothing. In many cases the identity *is* the clothing and image (can you imagine a middle aged lady in curlers and apron saying she is a punk? Or a pinstriped Rastafarian?). All sorts of subculture groups are recognisable by the fashion they wear: hippies, punks, teds, mods, skinheads, rastas, heavy metal freaks. In the words of musician George Melly, we have turned 'revolt into style'. Indeed, the main way the consumer society absorbs potential threats from subversive groups is to turn them into a new market for goods. It didn't take long before punk became an excuse for marketing more hair gel, saftey pins, zips and plastic bin liners – all the now familiar trappings of the 'punk' style.

When we are stripped of our consumer statements of who we are, we genuinely lose a sense of identity. In his book, *Beyond Identity*, Dick Keyes tells of his first day in the US army:

> Within a very few hours I was with hundreds of other men who were separated from their cars, clothes and hair. This created insecurity way beyond what I had imagined. Some compensated by telling stories about themselves that nobody ever believed. Others just withdrew in anxiety. Possessions can differentiate us from one another and establish our sense of individuality and thereby our value.[8]

This explanation helps explain two features of modern life: the shoplifter and the shopaholic. If some individuals can't afford to buy to prove identity they steal rather than miss out. The Government estimates that £1bn of stock is lost every year in the UK due to shoplifting.[9] The shopaholic is a person who goes on spending binges and becomes addicted to purchasing. According to Doctors Glatt and Cook of University College and Middlesex Hospitals, London, 'pathological spending' is an addiction comparable to drug and alcohol addiction. In the USA 'Shopaholics Anonymous' groups have been formed to help compulsive consumers kick the habit.

Needs and Wants

Many critics of consumerism – an odd alliance of Marxists, feminists, ecologists, Christians and Third World relief workers – have explained our society's addiction to consumer goods in terms of a distinction between real and artificial needs, or needs and wants. The priority, they say, is to meet everybody's basic needs before we can indulge ourselves in the luxuries of trashy consumer goods and the fripperies of fashion. They quote the words of Gandhi, that there is enough in the world for everybody's need but not for everybody's greed. The distinction can be illustrated graphically:

$$\frac{\text{TRUE NEEDS}}{\text{FALSE NEEDS}} \text{ or } \frac{\text{TRUE SELF}}{\text{FALSE SELF}} \text{ or } \frac{\text{THE NATURAL}}{\text{THE ARTIFICIAL}} \text{ or } \frac{\text{NEEDS}}{\text{WANTS}}$$

This sets up a dualism in modern society: there is a true self which we try to cover up by seeking false identities in consumer goods, and there are basic needs which we should ensure everybody has before we can buy our luxuries.

This dualism is the unstated assumption of most critics of consumerism, whether they be criticising it from a political, religious, moral, or other standpoint. However, there is a range of problems which this dualism causes.

Defining a 'natural' need

The dualistic assumption is that once a shared set of basic human needs have been met, people can go on to cater for their wants. But how do we decide what these basic needs are? Many people would say the basics are food, clothing and shelter. But where does this leave art, culture, religious faith, values, sex, democracy, physical exercise, literacy, human relationships – in fact all the things which make us fully human?

In the wants/needs distinction, most of culture would be relegated to second-class status. In reality, defining needs and wants becomes a matter of personal priority. I remember when a friend and I were both setting up home for the first time and discussing what he or I would buy with a limited amount of money. His list included 'basic needs' of setting up home such as a table, chairs and a settee. But my list of basic needs was quite different. I could not live in a house without pictures on the walls or shelving units for my books. There is no doubt in my mind – if I had to choose between a special picture on the wall and a settee, I would choose the picture. People could sit on cushions, stools or tea chests. My list of life's 'needs' was different from that of my friend. And what about another friend who is a professional artist? If nobody indulged in their 'wants' for good art he could not fulfil his vocation.

It all depends on your values. When Christ said that man shall not live by bread alone he was saying that our faith commitment is as fundamental – or more fundamental – to our lives as the food we eat. This priority was held by Uganda's Archbishop Janani Luwum as he confronted Idi Amin with the evil truth about Amin's actions. Luwum paid with his life because the outworking of his faith was more fundamental than life itself. Bishop Oscar Romero of San Salvador paid the same price, as did Sir Thomas More when he confronted King Henry VIII. Hunger strikers put faith or politics before food. Gypsies and many tramps choose to put freedom to roam above permanent shelter. Van Gogh, penniless, put his art above having money.

We never feel we've got beyond basic needs.

Few of us experience our own lifestyle as excessive and luxurious. We tell ourselves we *need* that car, blender, microwave, video player. Often, we feel we need them to do our duty as a parent or spouse. We need clothes. But how many do we need? A girl I know has around forty sweaters. When I asked her why she said she needed them for different moods, different occasions and so on. When she was on the forty-first sweater she still felt she was dealing with a basic need.

Needs vary from culture to culture

We are sometimes told about the pitifully low wages in some Third World countries. But in many of these countries they only need what we would see as a low salary to live a comfortable life. This is not at all to excuse exploitation of workers or meanness in giving to relief work, but simply to point out that somebody in a Third World country may be able to manage easily on a fraction of my salary. And, in a society where shopping centres are outside towns and few of us live near our workplace, most of us 'need' a car in a way people from other cultures do not. The answer is not just to sell our car but to persuade government, town planners, retailers and so on to operate according to different guidelines.

If my suggestion is correct that we use possessions to express our identity, then people in the West *do* 'need' a lot of their consumer gimmickry to hold onto a sense of identity. The answer is less to tell people to throw away the trash than to teach people to root an identity in more valuable sources, such as family, community, faith and a different set of values. An African in a village, surrounded by a strong wider family, sharing a clear set of values and believing life has an ultimate meaning is far 'richer' than a high-flying city yuppie who sits alone in the evening, watching videos and drinking. But the fact that there is so much urbanisation in Africa reveals – as well as a complex of economic causes – that so often we do not realise our own riches.

It means we romanticise the drab and mediocre

The logical conclusion of saying we need to cater for everybody's basic needs and not for wants is that everybody could happily live in bland, production-line housing and live on a diet of porridge and vitamin tablets. Like Kampucheans under the Pol Pot regime or Chinese under Mao we should all wear plain, functional dress and work in large, unaesthetic buildings.

It means we see the drab but adequate as some sort of ideal, believing this is somehow nobler. If you have £5 to spend on a haircut it is somehow nobler to have a short back and sides than a 'mohican', which is frivolous. But all cultures throughout history have produced art and literature, including turning people's bodies into works of art, believing that this too is fundamental to human existence. Culture matters and is not just an 'optional extra'.

It ignores the fact that fashion and ornament are valid aspects of identity

It is untrue to say there is a pure, untarnished self which can be separated from 'secondary' activities such as fashion, shopping, leisure, art, our furniture, and so on. All these things are entirely valid ways to express who we are, but become dangerous when they are elevated to being the only or main way we express this. Just as we all, to a certain extent, shape what we are to be more like our role models, friends, God or family, we express who we are through what we buy, wear, listen to and eat.

This is never clearer than in the case of fashion. The needs/wants people like to claim most fashion is silly, oppressive or a waste of money. Unquestionably, some of it is all of these things, but this view assumes fashion is the obsession of a deluded few. In fact it is a part of all of us.

Even being unfashionable is itself a fashion statement. It can say that you find fashion frivolous, oppressive, or that you don't consider clothes to be a high priority. Even counter-culture groups use clothes to make a statement about identity – in other words, they are involved in fashion. Desire for conformity is expressed by choosing the same image as those around you, non-conformity by choosing one which is different or more outrageous.

A particular feminist might denounce fashion as forcing a false role on women – but doesn't see her own dungarees and cropped hair as fashion. Or a preacher might denounce fashion as worldly, while he stands in cassock and dog-collar. Or an ecologist might say fashion is a mere want of a materialistic culture, while he stands in aran sweater and old cords. But each of these is using clothes as an expression of identity – in other words, they are using fashion. The only person who might conceivably be free from fashion (with a few exceptions – such as prisoners) would be naked and bald.

Linking the Private and Public Worlds

We have to express our identity somehow. There have to be some visible links between the private and public worlds. You can't opt out of that fact. We all wear clothes, buy food, most of us buy drinks toiletries, cars, magazines and we carry plastic shopping bags. We all like to feel we look reasonably attractive. But dualism induces a sense of guilt that all these are somehow 'artificial' activities.

My claim is that they are not artificial, but inevitable, and that each can be used in a good way or a bad way. Fashion is good when it accurately says something about the way I see myself and when it is a joyful experimenting in colours and shapes. It is bad when it exploits slave labour in Asian (or British) sweatshops or when an unwarranted percentage of our income goes on clothes (such as forty jumpers). Or when we try to buy into an image to compensate for a lack of a secure sense of identity or a lack of discernment.

In the words of a researcher for BBC TV's *Clothes Show*, Joy Wilson, 'A lot of people go around looking awful because they see an image in a shop or magazine which just doesn't suit them. They want to buy into that image, but it doesn't work.

People like that should be more critical in what they wear. They should experiment a bit more – a bit from Next, a bit from Oxfam, from Marks & Spencer and an antique clothes shop. Clothes should be about creating something uniquely you, they should be fun.'

The key to our use of fashion, furniture, cars, food and so on is that they are part of the items which make up your identity, but they are only a part of it. The others are the sort of areas outlined at the start of this chapter: family, spirituality, values, vocation and community. The sin of consumerism, the 'I shop therefore I am' mentality, is not that we impose a false self onto a true self. It is that we single out one aspect of identity and elevate it to the highest place above all the others. We allow one aspect of life to squeeze out other, vital elements.

An Alternative Model

An alternative model to the dualistic one is illustrated below:

fam	ily
spiri	tuality
val	ues
voca	tion
commu	nity
fash	ion
creat	ivity
ser	vice
hea	lth
shop	ping
compa	ssion
just	ice

More items could be added to this list. It is not intended to be exhaustive. It differs from the earlier diagram by drawing the dividing line in a different direction: vertically instead of horizontally. This is to show that none of the areas mentioned above is in itself artificial or wrong. They are all valid. But any can be used in a way which is good and life-enhancing or bad and destructive. It all depends which 'direction' you push it in. (For a further discussion of this type of model, see *Creation Regained*, by Al Wolters, Leicester: IVP, 1986, p 68.)

Family can be source of strength and belonging (and in an individualistic consumer society, can be a subversive unit which affirms the importance of relationships) or it can become tense and restricting. We can have good or bad values. We can be so obsessed with work that we shut off whole areas of life, or a vocation can be an upbuilding expression of talent and potential. We can deepen our sprituality in a way which explores the astonishing mind of the Creator or warp our spirituality so we try to find truth in horoscopes or the occult sections of bookshops, and we can become so spiritual in an 'other-worldly' sense that we neglect the God-given dimensions of relationships, aesthetics, nature, and so on. We can shop for goods which help Third World economies or ones which exploit them, use detergents which are kind to the environment or ones which pollute. Exercise can keep us trim and alert or it can become an obsession with our biceps which consumes all our energies and leaves no time for other activities. The 'direction' in which we push each of the aspects of our identity is crucial.

Furthermore, we can so unbalance our identity that we sever all but one expression of who we are. The rest of this book is about what happens to a culture which elevates one expression of identity – that of being a consumer of material goods – above all others, so that other expressions shrivel and die. It is the claim of this book that the consumer society has severed the most vital aspects of human identity, outlined at the start of this chapter, all of which centre essentially around relationships. It is only in rediscovering new dimensions to each of these that we can hope to combat the onslaught of the consumer world-view.

And it is about a society which pushes all the dimensions it does keep in the wrong direction, in a way which harms other people, the world around us and, ultimately, ourselves. It is about a people which sees the shopping mall as its true home, a people born to shop.

Notes

1 Andrew Morgan, 'Poll Shows British Teenagers Want Cash More Than Love', *The Times* 13 November 1987.
2 *Ibid*
3 Jeremy Seabrook, *'Stereotypes in Advertising'*, *New Society* 18 March 1988, p 12.
4 Quoted in Gaye Tuchman, Introduction, Gaye Tuchman, Arlene Daniels, James Benet (eds), *Hearth and Home: Images of Women in the Mass Media* (Oxford University Press: New York, 1978).
5 Tony Walter, *All You Love is Need* (SPCK: London, 1985).
6 Elizabeth Wilson, *Adorned in Dreams* (Virago: London, 1985).
7 Quoted in Robert S. Welch, 'Image and the 80s', *Focus on the Family* (USA January, 1988) p 6–8.
8 Dick Keyes, *Beyond Identity* (Hodder & Stoughton: London, 1984) p 104.
9 Home Office press release 27th April 1988.

3

MALL IS BEAUTIFUL

The Architecture of Consumerism

Buildings as Icons

After the Great Fire of London in 1666, Sir Christopher Wren submitted his plans for rebuilding London, including the design of the now famous St Paul's Cathedral. But at the centre of this new city stood, not the imposing classical dome of St Paul's, but the Bank of England and the Stock Exchange. Had the Fire taken place two hundred years earlier this would have been unthinkable. During the whole of the Middle Ages European life and architecture had been dominated by the church. The physical presence of the churches and cathedrals was a constant reminder of the church's influence in society. The church dominated not only your life but also the skyline of the city. By Wren's day something had changed.

Buildings, no less than paintings, can be icons. They say a great deal about the dreams and ideals of the culture and age which produces them. An ancient Egyptian writer described the city as the place where human beings 'put the gods in their shrines'. The city embodies an ideal. It takes a culture's highest visions, preoccupations and sense of ultimates and puts them at the physical centre of its life in the form of 'shrines'. Buildings say a lot.

By Wren's day the 'religious' buildings of the city were no longer the churches. They were the banks. In post-Reformation England it was the banks which reflected more accurately the ideals of the new capitalism sweeping Europe. Today too a visitor to the West could learn a great deal about the values we hold dearest by looking at the buildings which dominate our landscapes: the shopping megacentres and commercial tower blocks, temples of a consumer culture whose highest values are individualism, the creation and use of wealth and immediate gratification.

Origins of the City

Before 2500 BC the city as we know it didn't exist in the West. People lived off the land in small communities. From this background, the origins of the city were, above all, an expression of devotion, idealism and faith. In the words of historian Lewis Mumford:

> The first germ of the city, then, is in the ceremonial meeting place that serves as the goal for pilgrimage: a site to which family or clan groups are drawn back... because it concentrates, in addition to any natural advantages it may have, certain 'spiritual' or supernatural powers, powers of wider cosmic significance than the ordinary processes of life.[1]

The very origins of city life lie in an enlargement of village yearnings, aspirations and experiences. The city became an explosion of human energy. Personal preferences became permanent structures, personal ideals become shared customs and were given added force by the sheer numbers of people involved. If the city is the home of a god, people spared no energy in serving their god. Buildings were built to overawe with a sense of might or transcendence. Architecture became an expression of power and majesty.

The ideals and dreams of a culture are not incidental to the cities it builds and the structures it erects – they are the very source and motivation of these things. Probably the first culture to make the leap from village to city was ancient Sumer, around 2500 BC. The life in Sumer was centred around the king and the gods of the city. At the centre, towering above all life, was a massive, seven-storey system of terraced platforms called a ziggurat. The word ziggurat means pinnacle or summit and symbolised a mountain which bridged the gap between men and gods. At the very top was a shrine, the home of the moon god, where the Sumerian priest-king offered worship. The ziggurat was an architectural style common to the cities of ancient Mesopotamia, including Ur, home of Abraham, built around 2100 BC.

The grandeur of the ziggurat was wrapped around by a set of myths and gave dignity and awe to the culture's shared beliefs and social structure: at the same time it focused religious awe and bolstered the position of the ruler in society. He alone was allowed to enter the shrine. The ziggurat was a powerful symbol. In ancient wars the overthrow of the temple was taken as a symbol of destroying the very spirit of the people. Hence the significance of the biblical Tower of Babel, itself a form of ziggurat. As it is told in Genesis 11, the Tower is seen not simply as an exercise in building, but an act of self-glorification by its builders. The builders were not making a tower, they were making a statement.

The religious and idealistic focus of the city didn't die out in the following centuries. The Romans too saw the city as primarily a focus of myths and ideals. Before planning a new city they sought an augury – a kind of spiritual thumbs-up – from the gods. The tracing of the city outline was done by a priest and he guided the plough which began excavation work. As an anthropologist will tell you, if you can understand the meaning of the buildings, ceremonies and rituals into which a culture pours its energies, dreams and money, you can see some way into its heart, its values and system of priorities.

The Middle Ages

This can be seen in medieval Europe. The focus of cities, towns and villages was the church or cathedral. If the city was on a hill the cathedral would be at the top of the hill and the small streets of houses wound away downhill. The 'Mappa Mundi', or World Map, from Hereford cathedral, indicates cities by sketches of their cathedrals. The cathedral dominated the city not only by its physical presence but also by its rituals and routines. As Johan Huizinga describes in *The Waning of the Middle Ages*, in the absence of clocks and watches, the church bells marked every activity of life:

> One sound rose ceaselessly above the noises of busy life and lifted all things unto a sphere of order and serenity: the sound of bells. The bells were in daily life like good spirits, which by their familiar voices, now called upon the citizens to mourn and now to rejoice, now warned them of danger, now exhorted them to piety... Everyone knew the difference in meaning of the various ways of ringing.'[2]

The cathedrals are masterpieces of architecture. Bishop Reginald de Bohun, founder of Wells cathedral, insisted that the Glory of his God should be reflected in the glory of the churches: 'The honour due to God should not be tarnished by the squalor of his house.'[3] No expense and labour were spared in making them some of the most awe-inspiring pieces of art in mankind's history. They represented a pinnacle of many disciplines: architecture, engineering, glasswork, sculpture and even mathematics.

A pilgrimage to a cathedral, as described in Chaucer's

Canterbury Tales, was a highlight of life in the Middle Ages. Most people spent humdrum lives working on the land in their small rural communities. A pilgrimage to Chartres, Ely or Wells would offer a new vision of hope to a poor labourer, a brief respite from earthly troubles, a rumour of glory to come.

A key element in the splendour was the stained glass of the windows. These had the double purpose of giving a sense of mystery and beauty by filtering the light and acting as a teaching textbook. Filled with the stories of biblical characters and saints, the windows were a major way of teaching Christian truth to the uneducated, particularly since the mass was still held in Latin. But the teaching was secondary to the sheer emotional force felt on seeing the windows. Abbot Suger, priest at the church of St Denis near Paris in the twelfth century, described his experience of meditating on a particularly beautiful stained glass window as one of personal transformation:

> Then it seems to me that I see myself dwelling, as it were, in some strange region of the universe which neither exists entirely in the slime of the earth nor entirely in the purity of Heaven; and that by the grace of God, I can be transported from this inferior to that higher world.[4]

Because the cathedral was ultimately for God more than man, even the aspects invisible to the human eye had to be perfect. Fine sculptures and statues were placed where nobody would see them – except God, who would know the sweat which went into their production. It is true that in many cases the reasons for building the astonishing churches had as much to do with the desire for worldly displays of power by princes and bishops. But it was expressed in the grand language of faith, and the people of medieval Europe read the messages with the eyes of faith, seeing in the stained glass and candles not the ambitions of princes but the grace of God. It is also true that the cathedrals were frequently built amid poverty and squalor. But to accuse the church of theft or disregard is a misunderstanding based on the false needs/ wants distinction outlined in Chapter 2. People give all for their god. The churches, like other forms of art, were an expression of the shared core of people's faith, not a pleasant extra to be tacked on in times of affluence. And the churches embodied the one light in the drudgery of labour, one glimpse of a better way. Who would have sacrificed this for an extra crust on the table? And in any case the building of cathedrals was a source of major job creation, for workers ranging from unskilled labourers to skilled craftsmen, engineers and mathematicians.

Like the ziggurats of Mesopotamia, the cathedrals and churches of medieval Europe forcefully underlined the values of their culture. It is practically impossible to imagine building a cathedral on anything like the scale of Chartres or Ely today. Our dreams are no longer of St Augustine of Hippo's City of God on earth. Already the cathedrals of Europe stand like the strange statues on Easter Island: quirky and interesting, but people have forgotten what they might once have stood for. They remain as beautiful, imposing monuments to the faith of another age.

It may seem that in describing the Middle Ages in this way they could sound like a Golden Age, when Europe finally found a truly Christian civilisation. This would of course be an over-simplification. The world-view of a medieval peasant seems to have been a thick sandwich, the bread a bulky mix of local traditions, superstitions and pseudo-religious ideas, but the filling basically Christian. And this filling was at the heart of practically everybody's sandwich. Most people agreed on the major issues of belief and morality. Today, the filling has changed. For most people, Christianity is one of the many variables, a sauce which can be added or left off according to taste. Nor does it imply that if most people in Britain returned to the Christian faith, we'd necessarily embark on a pro-gramme of building cathedrals (or even churches!). Of course not. Each culture has its own, culturally relevant, ways of expressing its beliefs, including the architectural. My argument simply points out that the cathedrals embodied in stone something of the dreams and ideals of the culture which produced them.

When the Italian artist Canaletto painted a perspective of London in the eighteenth century, the architecture of faith still dominated the skyline. St Paul's dome stands tall, surveying the scene, while the rest of the cityscape is punctuated by the spires of countless city churches. There was no substantial change in the cities' skylines until the Industrial Revolution. This is underlined by Alec Clifton-Taylor, in *The Cathedrals of England*:

> Until the time of Queen Victoria the cathedrals were easily the largest buildings in England, if by size we mean area of space enclosed... Not until the development of iron and glass for building purposes were Englishmen to see still vaster spatial envelopes, structures such as the Crystal Palace and the splendid arched train-shed of London's St Pancras Station, the cathedral of the railway age.[5]

The Industrial Revolution

The new industrial age certainly had its cathedrals but they were cathedrals to a different ideal: that of progress through science, technology and human genius. After the French revolution in 1789 the revolutionaries for a while had designated the cathedral of Notre Dame in Paris a temple to Reason. The human mind was seen as the new saviour, pushing back the centuries of religious superstition and ignorance. The revolutionaries realised the importance of buildings as embodiments of ideals and so the architectural wonder already towering over the city was converted to the new creed. Something similar was to happen after the Russian Revolution in 1917, when churches were transformed wholesale into museums.

The British, less given to flamboyant gestures, allowed their churches to remain churches. But the same shift in ideas was taking place, and the shift found expression in architecture, seen most clearly in the vast building erected to house Queen Victoria's Great Exhibition of 1851 – the Crystal Palace. The Exhibition was the largest gathering together of industrial and scientific achievements the world had ever seen, and a building was needed to reflect the vastness of the undertaking. The Crystal Palace was a huge structure of iron and glass, and at 11,851 feet long it was large enough to hold nine cathedrals the size of Chartres. It housed 100,000 objects from 14,000 exhibitors around the world. Built in less than one year, its speed of construction and the overwhelming effect of seeing it were taken as symbols of the progress of Western culture and the conquering power of technology.

This point was felt strongly by Queen Victoria herself. She later noted in her diary:

> The sight... was so vast, so glorious, so touching. One felt – as so many did whom I have spoken to – filled with devotion, more so than by any service I have ever heard. The tremendous cheers, the joy expressed in every face, the immensity of the building, the mixture of palms, flowers, trees, statues, fountains, the organ (with 200 instruments and 600 voices...), and my beloved husband, the author of this 'peace festival', which united the industry of all nations of the earth – all this was moving indeed, and it was and is a day to live for ever.'[6]

The report in the Times went even further, commenting that some of those present 'were most reminded of that day when all ages and climes shall be gathered round the throne of their maker.'[7]

The religious aura was heightened by the effect of the glass. The queen called the building a 'fairy-tale palace', and the novelist Thackeray expressed the effect in poetry:

As though 'twere by a wizard's rod
A blazing arch of lucid glass
Leaps like a fountain from the grass
    To meet the sun!'[8]

This religious aura of peace, unity and devotion, was intended. Prince Albert, Queen Victoria's husband, underlined this aim in his opening speech: 'Nobody who has paid any attention to the particular features of the present era will doubt for a moment that we are living in a period of most wonderful transition, which tends rapidly to the accomplishment of that great end to which all history points, the realisation of the unity of all mankind.'

A passionate believer in progress through technology, Prince Albert saw the dawning of a new world, with England at the head. In his speech he referred to 'England's mission, duty and interest to put herself at the head of the diffusion of civilization and the attainment of liberty.'[9]

A visit to the Crystal Palace became a pilgrimage for people from all levels of society, joining together in a common celebration. It was the closest that citizens of a rapidly secularising society could come to the pilgrimage of Chaucer's day. They came to stand in awe and wonder at the noblest ideals of their civilisation, embodied in iron and glass. It was a pilgrimage of self-discovery, a glimpse into their own true identities and the faith of the age: they were part of humanity, with the role of subduing the earth and achieving universal brotherhood through progress. They were English, with the task of bringing enlightenment to the peoples of all races.

The railway boom of the mid-nineteenth century fulfilled a similar role. Trains, far from just being a quick way to get from Manchester to London, became symbols of the age of progress. Not all Englishmen were quite as obsessed by steam as the poet T. Baker, who saw the train as a form of salvation and the spread of steam abroad as a kind of evangelism:

Nor was this mania, this eccentric roar,
Confined to within Britannia's shore;
It made its way at that eventful time
To every land without respect to clime.
Vast were the schemes that now came forth in France,
Though not so wont in Britain's wake t'advance.
Europe was smitten to the very core,
And thence the mania raged from shore to shore...
Nay, e'en Van Diemen's Land and New South Wales
Determined, like the rest, to have their rails.[10]

But the mood he expressed was a common one. The railway symbolised progress. It was a foretaste of a unified humanity, bonded through science.

In this climate the stations became more than mere train-sheds. Their arches soared to the heavens, looking more like gothic cathedrals than functional, commercial units. The vaulted ceiling at London's St Pancras Station was the most spectacular of all. Its roof-span, a massive 243 feet, was the largest span of any roof in the world. The roof was supported by vast, soaring ribs – lending an air of dignity, grandeur, almost reverence. The builders of St Pancras were the Midland Railway. To make up for being late in building a London terminal for their lines, they decided to erect a building which would overshadow all other London stations, both in size and splendour. St Pancras was built not just to house trains, passengers and newspaper-stands, but as an object of admiration, a shrine conveying prestige and technical genius.

Shrines of the Consumer Age

Our age too has its shrines. The problem in recognising them is that it it is hard to stand aside from your own culture and analyse it with the sort of detachement that we apply to other ages and other cultures. We are a part of the culture, sharing its values and ideals. We look around us and see not great

buildings reflecting whole philosophies, but functional buildings which are there 'because that's the way things are'. To
identify the shrines of the consumer culture we need to go
back to the USA in the 1950s, origins of our current consumer
boom. The very earliest shopping malls, such as Northgate,
Seattle, were simply enclosed shopping centres under one
roof. By 1960 the term shopping mall was in common usage,
referring to a large, covered unit, containing dozens of stores
on the one site.

By 1988, shopping malls in North America accounted for 60
per cent of all retail sales, and 78 per cent of the population
went at least once a month. The malls dominate the landscape
for miles around, overawing by sheer size. They increasingly
dominate the lives of shoppers too. In 1960 the average visit to
a shopping centre lasted around twenty minutes. Today's pilgrimage to the shopping mall takes no less than an average of
four hours.[11] And the concept of the mall is already well established in the UK and is set to increase rapidly over the coming
years. Like the consumer culture itself, with its ideology formulated in America and exported round the globe, so too the
shrines of the culture are being erected in its honour. Look
around you.

A whole generation of American teenagers is growing up
describing themselves as 'Mall-Rats'. It is a generation whose
life revolves around the malls. The mall provides the setting
for leisure activities, relaxation, meeting friends, shopping
and window-shopping. America's young pop stars, such as
Tiffany and Debbie Gibson, play most of their concerts in the
malls, knowing that not only will the youth be there in droves,
but also the retail outlets for 'shifting product'.

Old people too sit and pass the time of day in the malls. The
mall, like the church in previous ages, has become the focus of
life. Once the church was the central point, claiming rights
over time, energies and creativity, and the market was a temporary, flimsy structure which came and went and was necessary for the most basic sustenance. Now the situation is

reversed. The shopping centre is the permanent magnet, drawing all forms of human life to participate. The church, conversely, appears on the scene to draw brief haloes over life's moments: birth, marriage, death.

Canada's West Edmonton Mall is the largest in the world. It boasts, at the last count, not only 828 shops and 110 eating places, but also a chapel. Now even the rituals of life and death can be performed, as life is lived, surrounded by shops.

Integral to the Mall is a mammoth theme park with wave pool, roller-coaster, submarines, dolphins, casinos, flamingoes, a life-size galleon and a fibreglass whale. Inside the mall you can enrol for classes in psychiatric therapy and care for your heart. If your legs get tired walking through the five-million square feet of shops you can hire Dan Dare-style electric tricycles to ride.

The emphasis in West Edmonton Mall, as with all the new malls, is on shopping as a leisure activity. The family can go shopping not simply to buy provisions and clothes – it is a complete day out. Shopping has become an activity to stimulate the imagination and excitement, as the soaring arches of gothic had done for the late Middle Ages and the vast, imposing ziggurat had done for the cities of ancient Mesopotamia. The fantasy element is completed by the fact that the mall is covered by a great glass roof, complete with artificial weather. Several malls have not only eternal summer, but a fake dawn and dusk. Life in the mall can be lived completely without reference to a real world outside. The American space agency NASA is using the self-contained shopping malls as a prototype for possible bases on Mars.

They keep on getting bigger and the figures get more staggering. The architect of the West Edmonton Mall, Maurice Sutherland, has plans for the ten-million square feet Fashion Mall of America, at Bloomington, Minnesota – twice the size of the West Edmonton Mall. American consumerism seems to be reaching the logical conclusion of the ideals it holds dear – life in a giant Disneyland of shops, lived under an artificial sun, where any aspects of life not centred around the accumulation and spending of money is considered irrelevant. It is a life spent sitting on Dan Dare tricycles, holding bags advertising your favourite store, your pocket full of plastic money, watched by enormous fibreglass whales.

Malls reach the UK

Meanwhile, the UK has been catching on. Despite the reluctance of many town planners to see malls on the US model in Britain, the rigorous logic of those holding the purse-strings of the consumer society has been prevailing. If all the applications to build new, large-scale shopping complexes in the UK went through, there would be enough to service 175 million shoppers, well over three times the total population of the country. In Britain, the construction of 'megacentres' has been described as the Third Wave of modern shopping. This follows Wave One – the hypermarkets of the 1970s, and Wave Two – the big DIYs and retail warehouses of the 1980s.

In 1980 the turnover from out-of-town retail parks was just £2.8 billion. By the end of 1988 it was £16.2 billion, and it was being estimated that by 1992 they would account for sales of £31 billion. Since 1980 their turnover has grown at a rate five times greater than the average retail sales. Following the American model, shopping centres are appearing with huge theme parks attached, to entice consumers to linger longer. The Meadowhall development near Sheffield, all one million square feet of it, boasts Europe's largest indoor water-park, aquariums, sculpture area, garden terraces, hotel complex and a leisure pavilion, featuring a snooker hall, ten-pin bowling, nightclub and fourteen-screen cinema.

The Metro Centre on Tyneside is another of the new edge-of-town UK megacentres turning to fantasy themes to draw in shoppers. They have invested in the help of a ten-screen cinema and the Enchanted Land of King Wiz, featuring the massive fibreglass King and his courtiers, including Whimsy the Dragon and Captain Swashbuckle. Metro Land, the theme park, is spread over 70,000 square feet on the first floor of the Metro Centre and cost £11 million. The theme park was designed by Forrec International, the Canadian company which designed and built the West Edmonton Mall. Already, according to a survey by Mintel market research, two thirds of Britons say they find shopping an enjoyable use of their leisure time. The designers of the new wave of British Megacentres intend to convert the remaining third. A survey by Gateshead Metropolitan Borough Council showed that visitors to the Metro Centre jumped by 45 per cent between May 1987 and May 1988, showing the attraction of the new leisure theme. Amusingly, the owners of the Metro Centre are the Church of England Commissioners, supposed bastions of another moral order.

The Bull Ring, which already dominates Birmingham city centre, is being updated into a massive new shopping complex of more than a million square feet, and a perimeter of more than a mile in length. Glasgow's Princes Square Shopping Centre is a £20 million complex covered by a huge glass dome. The largest building in Kent is a new Marks & Spencer warehouse. Even old rivals such as Marks & Spencer, Sainsbury and Tesco are dropping their rivalries to plant massive, combined out-of-town shopping areas. Next are moving out of town, and stores under the Sears banner are taking shoe retailing down the same road.

By virtue of their sheer size, megacentres such as Meadowhall and the Metro Centre become alternative town centres. They become a focus of time and energy, a site for regular visits, a meeting place. Even those modern cities which do not have malls and megastores yet tend to centre not around a monument, statue or church, but the shopping streets. Doesn't that sound suspiciously like the origins of cities such as Sumer at the start of this chapter? A friend of mine recently went to Dallas on a business trip. He asked his host where he could do some sightseeing.

'Sightseeing?' asked his friend, incredulous. 'There's nothing to see in Dallas. People just make money here.' The newly built city is a place which starts not by accident but as the embodiment of an ideal. It takes a culture's shared preoccupations and sense of ultimates and puts them at the centre of its life in the form of shrines.

Mega Problems

The significance of megacentres for Britain at the end of the twentieth century is not simply a symbolic one – that they represent the current national *consummania*. The aesthetic and social dimensions also have serious repercussions.

Even the designer of Tyneside's Metro Centre, John Hall, has expressed a concern that the new generation of megacentres will be architecturally second-rate: 'The quality will just not be there.'[12] The architectural writer Richard Porch expressed the same fear in the magazine *Design Week*. He foresaw a country studded with huge, bland sheds, designed not with an artist's eye but with an eye which stops at the cash-register:

> It is in this category of proposed out-of-town retail architecture that the true poverty of our vision is exposed, in the vast and unified schemes of this *genre*. The glazed-barrel vault, that unique 1980s contribution to the pantheon of design clichés, is to be found in super-abundance.
> The net effect of such mindless repetition is to produce a multitude of carbon copy perspectives all of which look like vapid imitations of some latter-day Great Exhibition structure time-warped from 1851.[13]

As megacentres become alternative town centres we increasingly centre human civilization around large, gaudy retail fish-tanks. Medieval Britain produced King's College

Chapel in Cambridge. Consumer Britain produced the out-of-town Tesco.

The social implications of megacentres are also serious, particularly for family life, the elderly and the housebound. Less than 40 per cent of women in Britain are car drivers and less than that have regular daytime access to a car. But transport is essential to reach the out-of-town sheds. So more and more women (who, statistically, do most of the family shopping) have to go at weekends when a car – and driver – are available. This eats into family time. Family life is becoming increasingly centred around the megacentres and there is less time for other family-based leisure activities. Shopping becomes your leisure activity whether you want it to or not.

Similarly, megacentres penalise the elderly and housebound. Once a village shopkeeper or the local grocer might have delivered to the old lady down the road and taken orders. They still do in the village near where I live. But the megacentre is distant – both geographically and humanly. The key word is no longer relationship but anonymity. Efficiency is all – pile up the goods and shift 'em quick!

Because of the focus on efficiency, service and the personal touch suffer. Most megacentres have the same, limited range of national chains, almost all catering for the under-forties, style- conscious consumer. The smaller, regional family stores are gradually being squeezed out of business. The UK already has the smallest percentage of small businesses in Europe – and that seems set to carry on declining as the big boys gobble up the smaller ones. At the time of writing, all except one of the national jewellery chains are owned by a single company.

Instead of Mr Robinson advising you on what fitting or screw to buy, you wander through alleyways of baffling oddments, unsure which to choose. Little provision of baby-changing areas, of loos or even seats for weary shoppers. No more personal counsel; instead, the blank stare of a checkout person, trained only to ask if you want to open a 'personal' account, unaware of the irony of the request. The word 'personal' is rapidly becoming meaningless as a result of over-use by retailers who use it to market the *im*personal, just as the word *natural* is used to market the *un*natural.

Many retailers and politicians are calling for government controls to balance the furious development of out-of-town shopping centres with the needs of existing town centres, in danger of disappearing under the 'doughnut effect' of stores abandoning the town centre and moving out to the edges. Perhaps we also need an official body to keep a watchful eye on the design and social consequences of the developments, a body which might dare stand in the way of retail 'progress' for the sake of a different set of ideals.

Concrete and Prince Charles

The chance to build can arise after a time of war or natural disaster, when buildings of earlier ages have been forcibly wiped away. The new buildings which rise from the ashes offer a glimpse into the values of the new age. The two decades immediately following the Second World War in Britain were characterised by a mood of optimism and idealism. A brave new world was to be built, a new world of prosperity and peace. Unlike some other European cities, which painstakingly rebuilt old buildings as they had been, London opted for a new start with architecture to match. Architecture was seen as a key part of the rebuilding and the job of piecing together a new London was given to William Holford, a leading architect of his day. Paternoster Square, a stone's throw from St Paul's Cathedral, was at the heart of the rebuilding.

Completed in 1967, the avant-garde walkways and towering glass and concrete blocks of Holford's Paternoster Square boasted affluence, power and success. The Square was featured in the opening credits of the 1960s TV series, *The Power Game*, a backdrop to tales of intrigue, glamour and money. By universal agreement, the rebuilding was a triumph, a perfect embodiment of the mood of the age. It said in concrete what Prime Minister Harold Macmillan had said in words: 'You've never had it so good!' It was not long before the once dominant dome of St Paul's was submerged amid the jostling, gargantuan tower blocks of the modern City.

There the cathedral remained, largely ignored by most of the employees working in the blocks, until December 1987, when Prince Charles reminded them of its existence in a widely reported speech. The Prince was speaking at a dinner of the Corporation of London Planning Committee. Why was it, he asked, that the great religious monuments of the past were obscured by blocks 'so mediocre that the only way you ever remember them is by the frustration they induce – like a basketball team standing shoulder to shoulder between you and the Mona Lisa'?

He also criticised the reconstruction of many of Britain's city centres after the war, all part of the 'rape of Britain'. Cities such as Coventry, Newcastle and Plymouth were rebuilt around consumer values – dominated by shops and finance blocks. The Prince put his finger on the issue when he said that the medieval buildings still left in London were 'dispossessed refugees' in the modern world. In an age where money talks, the medieval stones speak in a foreign language. The buildings of an earlier age stand awkward and homeless.

Many people agree with Prince Charles's views on architecture and the preference in the late 1980s is shifting to smaller buildings. People are recognising the value of human scale in architecture. Many of the new city centre developments are lower, less bland and less uniform than the 1960s blocks, but the mentality which produced 1967's Paternoster Square and cities dominated by finance towers, department stores and concrete shopping arcades has not been rooted out. It takes a firmer grip year by year.

Not that shopping is wrong, or that shopping in comfort or surrounded by leisure facilities is wrong either. If I can choose between shopping in a warm, pleasant environment and dingy, unpleasant stores, I will certainly choose the former. As I pointed out in the previous chapter, shopping in itself is fine, can be great fun and is an aspect of self-expression. But our culture has elevated this one dimension of life to the highest place so other values are squeezed out: we work to earn money to go shopping, we spend our leisure time shopping, we find our fun shopping, we silence our loneliness by shopping, we find our identity in our shopping purchases. We have less time for family and friends, culture, spirituality.

And we push this one dimension in an unhealthy direction. Art, design, human-scale planning, family life, the needs of the elderly, disabled and even the carless are dismissed. Small, family companies are squeezed out, the personal replaced by the impersonal. All that matters to the consumer society is the convenience of the affluent, mobile and style-conscious.

The New Shrines

Shopping malls, megacentres and commercial blocks are the temples of the new age. Speedbank machines are the wayside shrines where we perform our ritual devotions to the gods which motivate us. The icons which offered medieval people the ultimate choice in life have given way to the shelves offering the ultimate in consumer choices. The unified vision of society represented by a cathedral, temple or ziggurat has been displaced by a secularised dream of personal fulfilment, watched over by the benevolent gargoyle smiles of models on advertising posters.

In an earlier age life's adversity was met by a robust faith, even if it was only in human nature. Today we have our own solution. When the going gets tough, the tough go shopping.

Notes

[1]   Lewis Mumford, *The City in History* (Pelican: London, 1966) p 18.
[2]   Johan Huizinga, *The Waning of the Middle Ages* (Penguin: London, 1924).
[3]   Quoted in *Heritage of Britain* (Readers Digest Association: London, 1975) p 82.
[4]   Quoted in Painton Cowen, *A Guide to Stained Glass in Britain* (Michael Joseph: London, 1985) p 4.
[5]   Alec Clifton-Taylor, *The Cathedrals of England* (Thames & Hudson: London, 1967) p 9.
[6]   Quoted in J.R.C. Yglesias, *London Life & the Great Exhibition 1851* (Longmans: London, 1964) p 26.
[7]   Quoted in *Heritage of Britain op. cit.* p 302.
[8]   *Ibid.*
[9]   *Ibid.*
[10]   T. Baker, *The Steam Engine, Canto X*. Quoted in D.B. Wyndham Lewis and Charles Lee (eds), *The Stuffed Owl* (Dent: London, 1930) p 196.
[11]   Figure quoted in 'Satellite Shopland', *Equinox Factsheet* (Channel Four TV: London, 1987) p 27.
[12]   Quoted in Richard Porch, 'Mega Proposals', *Design Week* 27 March 1987 p 29.
[13]   *Ibid.*

4

NEVER-NEVER LAND

The Consumer Debt Trap

Easy Shopping

Let's face it, shopping just keeps on getting easier and easier, from haggling with bearskins through the development of coins and banknotes to cheques.

But today even the cheque book seems outmoded, overtaken by the small pieces of coloured plastic we call credit cards. Simply hand them over, sign your name and the goods are yours. But buying with credit cards still involves going into town, entering a shop and choosing goods. With the advent of shopping by post, buying has been made so easy you can do both the choosing and the paying from your armchair. And when you pay your bill by credit card, you don't even have to write a cheque – you just give them your card number and the sum is added to your monthly bill.

Meanwhile, the death-knell of the cheque book has been sounded. The Switch, Autocheque, Connect and similar cards automatically debit payment directly from your bank account each time you use them. To underline the success of the cards, Lloyds Bank have plans to take the experiment one stage further in a card of their own. Lloyds' card will also provide an automatic overdraft facility – all part of a general move by banks to ditch cheques and even credit cards in favour of a single, multi-purpose card. Barclays too see Connect as a stopping-off point on the road to a more comprehensive card. The days of the cheque book, like its counterfoils, appear to be numbered.

Easy Debt

While the trend towards simpler shopping has been going on, there has been another trend. This is the trend towards simpler credit – or, to put it another way: simpler debt. There was a day, which many still remember, when any sort of loan meant arranging to see your bank manager, the embarrassment of asking for a loan (akin to asking the girl in the chemists for a condom), and the stigma of knowing you were in the red.

Now bank managers trip over themselves in a pinstriped, lemming-like rush to lend you money. 'Please!' they beg you, 'let me lend you more! Car? Stereo? Certainly. How much would you like?' On two consecutive days recently I went into my bank, only to find myself ushered into a small side-room where a keen, balding man all but threw handfuls of cash across the desk. 'Remember, if you're ever in need of anything,' he ended by telling me, 'I'll be happy to arrange a loan.'

And borrowing has become easier thanks to bank credit cards. No need even to discuss an overdraft with a human being now. Buy goods with the card and delay payment for a few months. More and more High Street stores are joining in the game with their own store cards. A simple trip to a clothes shop has become a struggle to fight off enthusiastic young shop assistants, gleefully extolling the delights of 'personal accounts', 'instant credit' and 'delayed purchase deals'. With the removal in 1982 of minimum deposits on hire-purchase, debt became easier still. Before 1982, the buyer was forced by the deposit to consider the money he had, rather than relying on the money he might have in six months' time. But when compulsory deposits were abolished he could make a present purchase without any present consequence in his bank account. He could see the gain, but the financial loss was postponed to another day.

Sure enough, the trend towards easier borrowing has meant a massive increase in the problem of debt and its often tragic repercussions. Debt has become a national crisis. Stores and banks may claim debt only affects a reckless minority and that tinkering around with the system might help a few but would penalise the majority who use credit sensibly and responsibly. But these claims are hardly borne out by the statistics.

The Scale of the Problem

A major national study of credit and debt carried out in Money Advice Centres during 1987 by the charity Familybase showed that the average debt – of individuals who had sought money advice – was around £4,500, not including house mortgages. This figure tallies almost exactly with the figure given by the National Association of Citizens' Advice Bureaux, who are in the forefront of debt counselling. Familybase calculated that for these people, the average time it would take to repay the debts (at an optimistic estimate) is 10 years. It would take an unemployed person no less than 30 years to pay off all his or her debts.[1]

It is impossible to say exactly how many people are in the red, but there are certain indicators which illustrate the steep rise (a five-fold increase) in cases of debt between 1975 and 1986. In Britain today over half the households on Income Support are in debt (1.25 million), 1.5 million households are behind with fuel payments, and more than three quarters of a million people are more than two months in arrears on loans from finance houses. Half a million cases of personal (not including business) debt reach the courts annually, and the Citizens' Advice Bureaux receive a further 1.3 million debt-related inquiries each year (1987 statistic). In Autumn 1988 the CABs were announcing that they were 'close to saturation point' because of a rising tide of consumer debt problems.[2] The Office of Fair Trading were saying that three million adults had had difficulties in keeping up debt repayments during the past five years.[3] And in the USA, over 15 million households spend over half their disposable income in debt repayment.[4] Hardly a tiny problem.

Loan Sharks

As always where there is decay, the predators move onto the scene. The loan 'shark' has become a familiar sight, particularly in deprived inner city areas. Many are quite unscrupulous. Debt Counsellor, Sherree Smith, of the Birmingham Settlement Money Advice Centre, said some of the clients who came to her for advice had been paying annual rates of repayment of between 800 and 1,000 per cent (in other words, repaying the sum borrowed every six to eight weeks in interest):

> These particular credit companies are fringe operators, who go from door to door. When these ridiculously high interest rates are brought to our attention we can sometimes cancel them, if they are not in accordance with the Consumer Credit Act. But the fact remains that people who don't get advice from a body like ourselves go on paying these rates.

When people in the grip of these loan sharks default on payments, consequences can get nasty. Heavies are employed to break windows, doors and sometimes arms and legs. Dogs are brought round, rooms set on fire. In January 1988 four Glasgow moneylenders were imprisoned after it was proved that they had been charging a mind-blowing annual interest rate of almost 11 million per cent, and had taken possession of people's supplementary and child benefit books.

If an APR of 11 million per cent sounds impossible, think of it this way. If you have to pay back £5 on a loan of £10 by the end of the week, that is a weekly interest rate of 50 per cent. The following week, you will be repaying £15 plus 50 per cent interest, the following week £22.50, and so on. The sum snowballs, accumulating an ever higher sum of interest until the amount to be repayed bears no relation to the original sum borrowed. By the end of the year the theoretical sum would be several million times the original £10. Eleven million per cent APR is a weekly repayment of £2.50 for every £10 borrowed.

But such convictions are few. Most of the victims of the loan sharks are too scared to speak out and refuse to give evidence, even when there seems good chance of a conviction.

Pawn Shops

Until recently pawn shops still had a Dickensian image – relics of a former age, filled with dust and the jewellery of countless grannies. But pawn shops have moved with the times and since the Big Bang when the City of London became automated, have a distinctly yuppie air. They still keep their characteristic symbol outside – the three golden balls of the Medici family – but inside things are changing. Young city stockbrokers are pawning their sports cars and one recent customer pawned a helicopter for £20,000. The jewellery which still forms most of the shops' trade is distinctly 1980s.

The total number of pawn shops in the UK had dropped to 100 in 1982, but in debt-ridden Britain the total is at over 150 and set to keep on rising. The largest chain, Harvey-

Thompson, reported an income of £2.5 million in 1987. Pawning is effectively another form of credit. You receive instant cash against the value of your goods which are then held for six months before they are resold. During this time, interest is added on at around four per cent every month.

A New Problem

Unlike many problems which draw frequent condemnation from armchair 'experts' – such as alcohol abuse, assault and sexual immorality – the problem of widespread consumer debt is *not* one which in reality has always been with us. It is largely a new problem, a product of the late twentieth century consumer society. True, debt has always been with us, but this has been debt as a result of poverty. People ended up in debt just to stay alive. Now, we see large numbers of people getting into debt not because they have no choice, but because they want luxury goods which they see in shops and in advertising. A figure already quoted, but which bears repetition, is that between 1975 and 1986 consumer debt in the UK rose fivefold.

It is not a coincidence that the dramatic rise in debt has gone hand in hand with the rise of the credit culture, the culture which treats it as normal and acceptable that you are constantly exhorted to 'buy now, pay later'. It is a culture oiled by regular use of credit and store cards. Many of us still remember a day when buying on the never-never was frowned on. Now people who shun credit are aliens in the Never-Never Land we call the UK.

Between 1971 and 1986, the number of annual credit card transactions rose from just 10 million to an astonishing 451 million.[5] In the ten years between 1977 and 1986 the percentage of total consumer spending accounted for by credit virtually doubled (from 7.4 per cent to 13.6 per cent).[6] So what is the problem? Surely, using credit cards is simply another means of payment – an alternative to cheques or cash. The problem is this: most people don't use credit as a means of payment. They use it as a means of *delaying* payment. According to the large credit company Access, only 40 per cent of card users pay their bill promptly each month. The other 60 per cent delay payment for another day and pay interest in the meantime. And the signs are that people are tending more and more to buy on the never-never. Just during the year 1987, outstanding consumer debt rose by 18 per cent (from 30.8 billion to 36.4 billion). The National Consumer Council has described non-repayment of credit (credit default) as the most serious consumer issue of the 1980s.

Alongside the credit boom runs people's attitude towards savings. Quite simply, people aren't saving. The amount that people are saving is at its lowest since the late 1950s. In the fourth quarter of 1987, just 4.3 per cent of people's disposable income was being put in savings. As recently as 1980 the figure was 15 per cent. According to Christopher Smallwood of the Sunday Times, 'by the end of 1987, on average people were "dis-saving", using credit to spend beyond their income'.

It must be pointed out that people's financial assets in Britain as a whole are growing too. But assets tend to be tied up in a home. So, although your personal assets may be rising as your house price rises, these assets are not 'liquid', they are not readily accessible. A person would be reluctant to sell their house to pay off a £1,000 credit bill, so they take on more credit and loans. It also has to be said that the people with the houses are not always those who get into debt.

The Precipice

The picture is a disturbing one. Britain is a nation of consumers reluctant to save but increasingly keen to buy on credit, up to and even beyond what they know they can afford. A 1988 poster advertising Post Office National Savings was speaking to this mentality when it asked, 'Remember the days when you saved *before* you spent?'

People are walking along a dangerous financial cliff top. For many it takes only the slightest breeze to blow them over the edge into a turbulent sea of debts. Many are tragically drowned.

Spending more than you earn is glamourised as fun. At the economic level it is praised as patriotic because by consuming more you are creating more employment. An edition of the American *Sales Credit Journal* in the 1950s illustrated this by a modern-day parable: the tale of the wise and foolish lovers. The foolish lovers were so reluctant to incur debts that they delayed marriage until they had been able to save enough to cover all the costs of setting up home. Their folly, according to the journal, lay in postponing and missing out on life's pleasures. And in doing so they 'deprived the national economy of two or more years of family consumption'.

But the wise lovers, true citizens of the consumer culture, refused to be put off by lack of cash. They married, had a honeymoon on credit, bought a car on credit, took out a sizeable mortgage on a home, and furnished it on credit. True modern day heroes, they had what they desired instantly (why wait when simple credit terms can be arranged?), and they 'stimulated production, created employment, increased purchasing power, raised the standard of living'.

And there the parable left them. When I read this morality tale, it left me wondering what happened next. Did they live happily ever after? A few days later I discovered. I was reading my local newspaper when a story caught my attention. It was almost exactly the tale of the 'wise lovers', but transported from the world of Cadillacs and Elvis into that of Thatcherism and compact discs. A Cambridgeshire couple had married and had a baby soon after. Entranced by images of the good life, they had persuaded their bank manager to give them a mortgage of £70,000. They bought a car on credit and used credit and store cards to fill their new home with all the goods they had dreamed of owning.

It had not been long before initial payments of the mortgage and plastic cards were due. Unable to pay, they put off payment for another month. Interest was added on and when the next request for payment arrived it included the previous sum plus interest. The couple found themselves plunged in deep debt, a pit they could see no way out of. Unlike the moral of the hypothetical retail journal story, this true story was not one of wise lovers. It was one of dead lovers. Driven to utter despair, the couple had killed themselves and their small baby by directing exhaust fumes into the car where they sat, the car they were still paying for on credit.

Effects of Debt

Debt is a significant cause of suicide and attempted suicide, and it can cause a wide range of other serious problems. The Familybase *Families in Debt* report includes the results of in-depth interviews with 30 people in debt who had all been for debt counselling. The charity's researcher, Roberta Hanna, describes one case she encountered:

> One client (of the money advice services) discovered that he had debts when he returned home to find his wife unconscious after taking an overdose. The man's wife had been hiding the debt problems from him as he was recovering from a brain haemorrhage. She had eventually found herself unable to cope with the burden of mounting debt and so had attempted suicide as the only way out.[7]

Of course not all cases of debt problems get as far as attempted suicide. Five of the 30 interviewed by Roberta Hanna said they had felt suicidal. But mental problems are common. Of the thirty, twenty-eight were very worried, dreading the arrival of bailiffs and bills and in fear that the house would be repossessed. Many experienced sleepless nights and had sleeping tablets prescribed by their doctor. Most experienced an increase in tension. Some suffered physical ailments: a heart attack, high blood pressure and weight loss.

All those questioned said they had absolutely no social life. They couldn't afford to go out for a drink or meal or afford travel costs. Some said they had withdrawn from friends, fearing they would reject them if they found out.

One of the most serious effects of debt is on the marriages and family lives of those involved. Fourteen of the nineteen married couples experienced a great deal of tension in their marriage, which they attributed mainly to the debts. Two cases of divorce were directly or indirectly caused by debt, two wives left their husbands. In five cases couples admitted they would have split up over money problems if they hadn't been to a money adviser. A 'Mrs E' said:

> In the end we just split up due to it all. Every time another person or letter came to the door it was another argument.... It wasn't fair on the children. How the hell that little lass is sane I don't know because every night it was fighting, fighting, fighting.[8]

Another woman said: 'I think if it hadn't been sorted out, me and my husband wouldn't be married now. We couldn't stand each other'.[9] A Marplan opinion poll for the *Sunday Express* asked what people thought the main cause of family break up was. Sixty- eight per cent said money problems.[10] A representative of a West Midlands Citizens' Advice Bureau, in the frontline of debt counselling, told me that the major tragedy about debt problems was that they never remained in isolation:

> Debt always has major repercussions on the families of those involved, particularly if there is unemployment in the family as well. It affects a couple's marriage, because they are always in the house, on each other's backs. Any little problem is immediately magnified. The home, which can be a place of support, becomes

an inhibiting, explosive situation. The parents get depressed because the family has labels of being poor attached to it, such as free school meals. And there's no money for holidays, telephone calls or trips, so it becomes hard to keep in touch with grandparents who live any distance away. Because of this, relationships with the wider family suffer as well.

Little wonder, then, that the Bible speaks of debt as a kind of slavery:

> The rich rule over the poor and the borrower is servant (slave) to the lender (Prov 22:7).

or that Christ himself uses debt as the ultimate analogy of sin and forgiveness when he teaches his followers to pray 'forgive us our debts as we forgive our debtors' (Mt 6:12), and in the parable of the unmerciful servant. On both sides of the analogy – debt and sin – justice imposes a burden of obligation which overshadows all else in life, but requires mercy to be shown. Sadly, the area of debt is one where mercy is rarely in evidence.

It would be easy to throw up one's hands in resignation faced with the facts of debt. It's just another aspect of the modern world. Times change. These things happen. But the massive amount of hurting in the West which can be blamed on debt cannot be shrugged off so lightly. We need to ask why people are taking on ever greater credit and borrowing commitments and toppling over the cliff in ever greater numbers.

Causes of Debt

The answer lies in a combination of a greater willingness on the part of the stores and lenders to lend, and a greater consumer desire to borrow. Firstly, the lenders. High Street stores are noticeably keener on 'buy now pay later' selling than in the past. When Owen Owen, he of department store fame, arrived in Liverpool in 1865, he had no doubts as to the role of credit: 'The guide to the harbour of best success is to give no credit to anyone for longer than two months.' How times have changed. As I write, the windows of the Liverpool branch of Owen Owen declare: 'Up to £1,250 credit to spend immediately' and the store is charging an interest rate of 34.4 per cent per annum.

Sir Gordon Borrie, Director General of the Office of Fair Trading, accused stores of giving away their in-house credit cards 'like sweeties'. Marks and Spencer has 2 million card holders, the Burton Group 2.8 million. Research by the Debenhams store carried out in 1982 showed that customers paying by card spent around twice as much as cash customers.

As a result, the stores are doing all they can to attract credit buyers. Some High Street stores have taken to showing just the monthly repayment sum on electrical and other goods, instead of the actual price. Sometimes their tactics leave less room for free will. In 1986 the Burton Group insisted its 37,500 employees join its credit card scheme if they wanted to claim their staff discounts. These discounts are an important perk for shopworkers, some of Britain's lowest paid employees. In April 1988 House of Fraser's 16,000 workers were told they would no longer receive their discounts unless they joined the company's Frasercard, and 40,000 workers at Sears stores (which include Selfridges, Dolcis and Freeman Hardy Willis) were given a similar ultimatum. When the shop-workers' union, USDAW, heard of House of Fraser's move, it wrote to the store, pointing out the danger of 'encouraging credit for staff who are often very low paid'.

According to the Monopolies and Mergers Commission, the clearing banks' credit card operations are the most profit-able part of their operations. More credit shifted, higher pro-fits.

The availablity of loans has also increased. Dr Andrew Hartropp, lecturer in Financial Economics at Brunel University, pinpoints two developments at national level which pushed this process:

> First, the relative decline in lending in the 1980s both to Third World countries and to UK industry may have led the lending institutions to put more effort into the personal lending market in the UK. Secondly, since 1980 the Conservative government has been dismantling many of the controls and restrictions on the financial institutions, especially regarding lending to households. This deregulation of financial markets may have unleashed large amounts of funds for consumer lending which had previously been artificially restrained.[11]

But greater willingness to lend by itself would not account for all the changes. People had to be willing to take on greater credit. There had to be a shift in mentality away from the 'old-fashioned' attitude that debt was shameful and that instant gratification was less worthy than patience and saving. The onslaught on the West's residual puritanism began in 1950s America. Advertisers and salesmen sought to persuade consumers that if you fancy it you should buy it – now. It seems to have worked. During the 1950s consumer debt in America rose three times as fast as personal income. Extensive research in the early 1960s by the Chicago Tribune newspaper confirmed that the consumer credit mentality had permeated all levels of US society:

> There has been a shift from the philosophy of security and saving to a philosophy of spending and immediate satisfaction... more self-indulgent spending, a tendency to equate standard of living with possession of material goods...'[12]

Britain seems to have been slower to join the brave new world of consumer credit, but by the early 1980s was a fully-fledged Never-Never Land too. We had been told that buying with credit 'takes the waiting out of wanting', 'gives you instant buying power', it 'opens doors', that 'now there is an easy way to turn your dreams to reality'. Hundreds of thousands of credit cards were sent through the post to customers who had never requested them. Television adverts for personal loans showed the figures on a car price tag rapidly diminishing to stress how affordable the car could be with a bank loan. The banks' advertising budget for credit card promotion in 1986, on TV and in the newspapers, was £16.7 million. This does not include the amount spent on 'junk mail', in-bank publicity and promotions through free gifts.

When we advise children on money matters the issue at stake is not so much whether credit is a good or bad thing, but how we should teach children to use it. If the adult world of plastic money and bank accounts was once viewed with studied indifference by children it is now seen as part of their territory. High Street banks offer an array of bank identity cards, secret codes, badges and other paraphernalia. In August 1987 Linda Saunders opened the Young Americans Bank in the USA, where minors could have bank accounts and even take on credit to pay for dolls' houses and bikes. The French bank Credit Agricole has opened some 3,000 'kiddy cash dispensers', where children can draw on up to £200 a week on their own special credit cards. After all, let them start the way they mean to go on.

Credit has become a way of life for most of us, an aspect of living which we never really question, until something goes seriously wrong and your flexible friend turns out not to be so flexible or so friendly after all. The fact that the evidence indicates debt is particularly focused among younger people underlines the blasé attitude which those growing up in Never- Never Land have towards credit and loans.

Getting into Debt

So how exactly does taking on a large amount of credit result in debt? Many people in debt were not the reckless spendthrifts you might imagine, so intoxicated by images of the good life that they spent far beyond their income. On the contrary, most people do make some attempt at balancing their personal budget, but the danger is that they sail too close to the wind. They spend or commit themselves in credit too close to the full amount of their income, without keeping a 'nest-egg' in case of emergency. This leaves them vulnerable to the slightest change in personal financial status. A family member may lose overtime pay, the wife may become pregnant and have to leave her job, there may be an unexpected car repair or a hole blown in the roof during a gale.

Any of these is enough to tip a person over the edge. Then, once payments are delayed to the next month, interest is added on and the debt increases. According to Dr Andrew Hartropp, 'Once income falls behind outflow, then debts build up, interest payments accelerate and to climb back only to the very edge of stability becomes hard if not impossible.'[13] At this stage, people are tempted by newpaper advertisements which promote loans to repay all your debts in one go. They often do not realise that if they are having trouble with several small loans, they will have even greater trouble with one big loan, which is likely to have a very high rate of interest. Others turn to loan sharks.

Particularly vulnerable are those on low incomes, and it remains true that debt tends to affect poorer families more than the better off. But, according to Joan King of the Peacehaven Money Advice Centre on England's relatively prosperous south coast, it is a myth to see debt as solely a problem for the poor or those in the industrial north:

A large number of affluent southerners are ending up in debt. They are being encouraged to take out loans, and then when their circumstances change they find they can't pay. A northern money adviser recently said to me, 'Down South you don't know what it's like', but I said hang on, we have different problems – the problems caused by affluence, such as higher house prices. People are buying houses they can ill afford. And if people don't buy big houses, they may have to buy cheaper properties which need money spent on them. Wages are high if you are in work, so advertisers say, 'You've got a high income – buy another car'. We also have a higher rate of credit card use. Card companies tend to blitz southern areas, and that can lead people to making big purchases on credit without counting the cost.

The credit culture shows every sign that it will continue unabated, at least for the immediate future. As for the long term, a note of warning comes from a company called Industrial Market Research, who warn that eventually the use of personal credit will slow down. The reason? We shall all be so worried about our debts. This is one of the conclusions of a 200-page report, 'Business Opportunities in the Company Credit Card Market'. But I wouldn't recommend you buy a copy to examine the whole argument. It costs £9,700. Plus VAT.

Action on Debt

In the face of a massive credit boom and growing debts, what should be done? Action is necessary both at individual, group and national levels. Firstly, each of us can take several steps to make sure we do not fall into the debt trap:

▷ Budget to ensure that income always remains well above outgoings. Think of the worst likely circumstance (for example, a rise in the mortgage interest rate) and make sure you could repay.

▷ As far as possible, keep a 'nest-egg' of savings in case of unexpected emergency.

▷ Use credit sparingly and always pay your monthly bill on time.

▷ If you intend to take on a store card, shop around for the lowest APR (annual percentage rate of interest). These currently range between 19.5 per cent and over 40 per cent.

At group level, teaching on money has been a neglected area in schools, youth groups and churches. Solid teaching on the dangers of debt might save many from being wrecked when they hear the siren-call of 'buy now pay later'.

Action should also be taken at government level. Economic safeguards are needed in a similar way to the safeguard of seat belts in cars, to help prevent possible tragedy.

One area in urgent need of control is interest rates, which are extortionately high in the UK. It seems almost everybody agrees on this except the credit companies themselves. In January 1988 the National Consumer Council reported that interest rates on bank credit cards were far too high. And this report did not even include the far higher rates on High Street store cards. These store cards were referred to by *The Guardian* as 'the great High Street rip-off', and they prompted Roger Carroll in *The Sunday Telegraph* to remark: 'Never in the history of human credit have so many people been overcharged so outrageously.' In the USA, rates vary from state to state, but all rate ceilings on credit cards are between 18 and 24 per cent, only rarely going beyond 20 per cent.

High interest rates are responsible for pushing people deeper into debt because of high monthly charges. According to the director of Familybase, economist Dr Michael Schluter, none of the three possible reasons given by the credit companies for the high rates is adequate:

▷ *The stores operate credit very inefficiently, so they need the high margins to cover overheads.* But if this is true, why should Britain be less efficient than other countries, and why should the British consumer be expected to pay for this inefficiency?

▷ *There is a high default rate.* But if so, considering the agony to individuals and families caused by each case of bad debt, if lenders have a high rate of customer default they should be more careful about lending than they are at present. This also means that reliable borrowers are subsidising unreliable ones.

▷ *Lenders are making massive profits*. The clearing banks' credit card operations are the most profitable part of their operations. Given the much higher rate on store cards, it is possible that their rate of return is substantially higher. The deluge of media and direct mail advertising promoting credit suggests very high profits are being made in the industry. If so, it is wrong that these profits should be made at the expense (literally) of people already in debt, who are being pushed deeper into debt by the high rates.

Dr Schluter suggests an overall limit of 50 per cent, with High Street rates not above 20 per cent. In February 1988 the House of Commons approved Elliot Morley MP's Credit Control Bill to tighten credit laws, which included a ceiling on interest rates. Mr Morley said the Bill was to help alleviate the price of personal credit, a 'misery which hangs round people's necks like a chain'. It was given an unopposed first reading but did not go any further because of a lack of parliamentary time. A bill such as Mr Morley's is urgently needed.

It must be added that the one exception to the high rates is the John Lewis Partnership. The stores in the partnership have a store credit card but use it strictly as a service to customers rather than a way of making high profits. Its interest rate is just 19.5 per cent, while others hover between 26 and 40 per cent. Lewis's proves that Dr Schluter's call for a ceiling on interest rates is workable and in the best interest of customers.

So why do rates remain absurdly high? There are two parts to the answer. Part one is that high rates mean big profits. The second was expressed by a spokesman for a leading High Street electrical retailer, interviewed alongside myself in a debt article in the *Universe* newspaper: 'Companies *do not have a responsibility* to the consumer to bring down high interest rates.' In other words, if people suffer as a result – tough.

The Ethics of Debt

This is quite a contrast from the view taken of interest in the Old Testament Law. While all the countries around Israel happily charged interest on loans, there was a strict ban in Israel on interest on loans to fellow Israelites:

> Do not charge your brother interest, whether on money or food or anything else that may earn interest (Deut 23:19).

The biblical word sometimes translated 'usury' or 'excessive interest' simply refers to all interest. For more than the first millenium of its history the church too banned usury, seeing it as a destroyer of relationships and an act of oppression, particularly of the poor. The Roman Catholic church officially opposed interest until as recently as 1854. Even when Calvin stated that he saw no reason why interest in itself was bad, he was still at pains to stress that it was wrong to take interest from the poor or neglect their needs. In the words of Dr Hartropp, 'Transactions must be for the common good not simply for the individuals involved... Calvin saw the importance of government intervention without which economic harmony could not reign.'[14]

Among the many powerful biblical passages linking usury with exploitation is that of the prophet Ezekiel:

> Will you judge this city of bloodshed? Then confront her with all her detestable practices and say, 'This is what the sovereign Lord says... you take usury and (excessive) interest and make unjust gain from your neighbours by extortion...' (Ezek 22:3, 12)

Dare we suggest that in our supposedly sophisticated consumer society, we actually have a less sophisticated view of usury than centuries of saints and prophets? At the very least, we need to listen again to the voice of Ezekiel in a Britain where extortionate rates of interest are commonplace.

Another area of concern is the way credit is promoted. Current practices include schemes similar to trading stamps, where you gain one point for every £10 spent and you can trade in points for more goods. Several banks and building societies have issued 'charity' credit cards, which promise to give a donation to a prominent charity when you first take on a card and then for every £100 spent using it. A finance company offered a £500 holiday voucher to clients taking out a £3,000 loan. Such practices are irresponsible because beneath a veneer of charity or prudence, they encourage reckless overspending on credit.

Many people are getting into trouble because they do not understand the jargon of credit promotion. Terms such as APR or 'secured loan' should be clearly explained. And why not a government health warning, like we see on cigarette advertising? Beware, credit can seriously damage your health!

The British Government has started to take a step in the right direction on this matter. In March 1988 the Corporate Affairs Minister Francis Maude told the Institute of Credit Management that by the end of the year he wanted to see explanations on adverts, including a warning on 'secured' loans that this meant your house was on the line. 'All too often, consumers are misled by advertisements offering credit facilities. My intention is to make sure these advertisements are as simple as possible so that consumers clearly understand the consequences of entering into a credit agreement,' he said.

Advice centres, such as the money advice centres and the Citizens' Advice Bureaux, are overrun with debt counselling needs. The centres do an excellent job helping debtors set income against expenditure, look at the balance and sort out priorities. They make phone calls and help draft letters to lenders and in many cases are the only barrier between the debtor and suicide or family break-up. Many offer the free services of a local solicitor who advises on the legal aspects.

But these centres are grossly underfunded. According to Anne Andrews, Development Officer of the Birmingham Settlement Money Advice Centre, there is a national shortfall of 96 per cent in the provision of money advice for those in need. A percentage of credit company profit – perhaps just half of one per cent of the total monthly credit taken on by consumers – should go to fund debt counselling.

To these could be added the reintroduction of compulsory minimum deposits on credit purchases, so that you at least have a portion of the cost to reckon with on the day you buy.

One thing is clear: reassessment at personal level and action at national level is vital if situations like the following are to be avoided. These are two letters I received from readers of a newspaper article I wrote on debt. The first was from an elderly lady who told me of her sense of imprisonment because of her debts:

> I'm glad you wrote – someone had to. It's the credit cards that has me in their grip, more than the catalogues, only they all add up together and the bills seem to arrive together too.

She said she had reached the stage where she was having to sell more and more of her goods to meet her credit repayments, and had realised that credit was not the benefit she had thought:

> I've got a lot of cacti I'd like to sell, but who wants them? I've been growing them for many years, quite a lot from seed. It's when the people offering goods put that word 'only' that gets me, this or that is 'only' this amount. It sounds good, but now I've realised it isn't good, so now I don't buy anything but just concentrate on trying to pay off the amount every month, only it means another year when I won't be able to afford a holiday...

The other writer told me of her conviction that credit and loans were too readily available and of her own descent into debt:

Credit ruined my marriage, my self-image and our family's future. It was a dreadful spiral which almost led to the loss of our home.

She wrote of her first application for credit, to pay off her overspending on Christmas presents, her amazement at how easy it was, and how pleased the company were to help her hide the loan from her husband:

Not only did I get it (cash in hand the following day!) but they also agreed to use my office address rather than my home address, so the deception began. From time to time they offered me further funds which I was too weak to refuse and I had, by that time, also contracted with various stores for credit card debts as well. Soon it was completely out of control and I had to borrow further just to meet the monthly repayments.

She said the worse the problem became, the harder it was to tell her husband the truth. It was only when she was close to mental breakdown that the truth came out. The story has a happy ending, because in desperation she turned to the church in which she had been baptised fifteen years earlier. The pastor and treasurer took charge of the finances and organised affordable repayments with the creditors. She still has at least ten years of repayment ahead of her. The care of the church also led to a rediscovery of the faith in God she had lost some years earlier.

But, as she told me, the wounds inflicted on a relationship would take longer to heal:

The most awful thing to deal with is the lack of trust and forgiveness towards me by my husband, but who can blame him? Debt turned me into a deceitful liar from an honest, trustworthy person.

For countless others, debt is a trap which they can see no way out of, a place without hope and without healing. As my correspondent concluded:

> Whatever I hear about people's shortcomings these days my reaction is 'there but for the grace of God go I'. It's so easy to fall into the debt trap. Let's make it harder to fall in and easier for them to climb out.

Notes

1. *Families in Debt* (Jubilee Centre Publications: Cambridge 1988).
2. David Brindle, 'Debt Queries Swamp CAB', *The Guardian* (26 September 1988).
3. David Churchill, 'Credit Providers Urged to Act on Debt Problems', *Financial Times* (7 July 1988).
4. Figure from Griffith Garwood, 'Consumer Borrowing in the US', *Money and the Consumer* (Money Management Council in association with American Express: London 1988) p 97.
5. Figure from *Familybase News Debt Trap Special* (Jubilee Centre Publications: Cambridge 1988).
6. Figure from Economic Trends Annual 1987 (Central Statistical Office: London 1987). According to a major international study carried out by Mintel in May 1989, Britain owns far more credit cards than any other country in Europe.
7. *Families in Debt op cit.*
8. *Ibid.*
9. *Ibid.*
10. Marplan Survey, *The Sunday Express* (August 1988).
11. Andrew Hartropp, *The Debt Trap* (Jubilee Centre Publications: Cambridge 1988).
12. Quoted in Vance Packard, *The Waste Makers* (Penguin: London 1960) p160.
13. Andrew Hartropp, *op cit.*
14. *Ibid.*

5

UNSPORTING ACTIVITIES

The Commercialisation of Sport

Entrepreneurs in Training Shoes

When Jimmy Connors quipped that going onto the tennis court to play a game was 'just another day at the office,' he actually said more about sport today than he might have realised.

Top sportsmen and women today are also top business people. High-level sport has long since ceased to be the province of gifted, enthusiastic amateurs. It has become a money-spinning multinational industry and, as such, has attracted a mass of hangers-on who care more about big bucks than bats and balls. The stakes for winning and losing are no longer measured just in terms of fame and biceps. They are measured in pounds, dollars and yen.

When Stefan Edberg won the 1988 Wimbledon Men's Singles final he netted a tidy £165,000 in prize money, not to mention the spin-offs in terms of sponsorship. Steffi Graf, Women's Singles champion, won £148,000. All players at Wimbledon, however successful or unsuccessful, were given a

£50 a day 'poverty allowance' to cover expenses. In today's Wimbledon, players who are knocked out in the qualifying rounds are paid more than the £2,000 Rod Laver had for winning the Men's Open title twenty years ago. Any of the world's top fifty golfers can earn in a few months what a professional golfer would have taken a lifetime to earn up to twenty years ago.

In our cash-obsessed society, the news-angle in stories on the sports pages of newspapers is frequently the prize money. This is even true in less obviously commercialised sports such as squash. Norman Norrington, manager of Europe's number one squash player Del Harris, acknowledged that sport was about cash – lots of it: 'The money is staggering. The people in the bank are already calling him sir.'

The mind-boggling sums of prize-money which are starting to creep into certain sports have become inseparable from other sports, such as boxing. The 1988 World Heavyweight Championship fight between Tyson and Spinks grossed over $75 million. Of this, $22 million went to Tyson, $13.5 million to Spinks.

In the same year, Sandy Lyle became the first golfer to be told he had simultaneously won £1 million in prize money in Europe, and a further $1 million in America. And when Nick Faldo and Curtis Strange battled it out amongst the tees and caddies in the US Open, they were playing for £100,000 (a mere £50,000 for the runner up). Later in 1988 the Welsh golfer Ian Woosnam became the first golfer to win £1 million in prize money for one single tournament, played in South Africa.

Although athletes are still nominally amateurs, appearance fees ensure many a runner and jumper a jolly little earner. The manager of Canadian sprinter Ben Johnson, Larry Heidebrecht, was insistent in June 1988 that Johnson would not race against Carl Lewis. That, at least, was until Johnson was offered $250,000 for the 10-second race. Heidebrecht admitted: 'The money offer changed my philosophy. It is substantial.'

Cash and the Olympic Ideal

The lesson of our consumer society is that money can do just that – it can change people's and institutions' philosophy. More about that in the final chapter, but for now it is worth mentioning the Olympic Games in this respect. Until the 1984 Los Angeles Olympics, no government expected to profit materially from the Games. Spin-offs came in the form of international prestige and attention. With Los Angeles that all changed. Through sponsorship the Games made a huge profit.

McDonalds paid $9 million to be the 'official Olympic fast food', Coke paid $15 million to be the 'official soft drink'. Not a lot to do with sport, international harmony or health, but extremely healthy for the coffers. The pattern was repeated at the Seoul Olympics four years later. Coke kept its place as official fizz, and Visa joined in as the Games' 'official payment card'. By worming its way into the Olympic ideal, advertising has reached the heart of a previously hallowed arena of non-professional, non-commercial idealism.

The sponsors all see their involvement as a link with a symbol of integrity, quality and health. The International Olympic Committee (IOC) has a marketing agency, International Sport Leisure Marketing. According to Andrew Craig of the agency, 'Essentially we are selling the good, clean Corinthian image of the Olympic games.' The athletes commission of the IOC have already held meetings to discuss the possibility of Olympic prize or appearance money, a proposal held by many of the committee members to be a serious possibility for the future.

In the ancient world, from 776 BC onwards, warring Greek states gathered every four years in Olympia to put feuds temporarily on one side. The Games celebrated the human body, harmony between nations and the gods, in whose honour the events took place. The ideals of fitness and harmony linger, but the gods we honour through the Games have been updated: commercial success and prosperity.

When Ben Johnson was stripped of his gold medal at the Seoul Olympics for drug-taking he lost out on an estimated £15 million over the following four years. Johnson was told immediately that he had lost £3 million in sponsorship from various companies paying through the nose to have the sprinter's name associated with their goods. The companies included the Italian sportswear manufacturers Diadora (who tore up a £1.6 million deal), Mazda cars, Toshiba, Johnson Wax and Timex. The Finnish co-op, Valio, scrapped a TV commercial for milk which featured Johnson, for which he would have been paid around £80,000. Following the Olympics the USSR joined France and West Germany in giving cash hand-outs to their gold medallists. Before the Games a Filipino businessman, Lucio Tan, offered a free home and £30,000 to the first gold medallist from his country.

For many people the Johnson affair was their first glimpse into the world of big bucks behind international sports personalities. The stakes are frighteningly high. Little surprise that top athletes and gymnasts take the risk of illegal performance-enhancing drugs and force their bodies to become unnaturally distorted sport machines. The pressure is to win at any cost.

Soccer

In the Summer of 1988 there was the threat of a breakaway 'Super League' from the English Football League. This would have been composed of twelve or thirteen of the top clubs, who would have played against each other outside the old League. The proposals came from Independent Television, who offered generous sums for exclusive rights to cover the League. It would have meant the end of soccer in the UK as we know it. As such, it is a prime example of commericalism not simply supporting sport by helping it make ends meet, but calling the tune. If the plan had gone ahead the decision would have been taken not so much coolly, and in the best interests of the game, but with the prospect of cash in hand.

The Football League, according to Ken Jones in the sports pages of *The Independent*, needed space to plan the future of football without pressures of this kind. It 'was crying out for leadership without the whiff of entrepreneurial manipulation'. There was an equally strong reaction from within the game, as players and managers understood the motive for the proposed changes. The Chairman of Coventry City FC, John Poynton, said, 'It is an idea that smacks of Judas money, based on pure greed.' Gordon Taylor, Secretary of the Professional Footballers' Association, echoed the same feelings: 'People say we're in a Wall Street game. In our centenary year, it's an absolute disgrace.'

Cricket

If the proposed Super League had gone ahead, it would have caused a similiar revolution in soccer to that which one man had caused around ten years earlier in cricket – Kerry Packer. Packer was a businessman who approached the Australian Cricket Board (ACB) for the exclusive TV rights for cricket for his Channel Nine television network. When the ACB turned down the application, Packer decided to go ahead with his own televised cricket spectaculars anyway. The ACB would continue without the players poached by Packer.

Under the name of World Series Cricket (WSC), he gathered around 50 of the world's top cricketers for 'superstar' matches. The feel of the matches was quite different from cricket as it had previously existed – a calm, gentlemanly game played at a gentle pace, often over several days. The mood of the Packer game is summarised by the BBC cricket commentator and editor of *Cricketer* magazine, Christopher Martin Jenkins:

> In order to drum up publicity and television interest, the organisers of WSC encouraged such things as open discussion of prize-money, obtrusive advertising, showbiz style playing to the gallery, and gamesmanship. Cricket was presented to its 'new' public in Australia not as a subtle, profound and skilful exercise, but as a game of blood and thunder played by larger than life characters in coloured clothes. The commentators on Channel Nine were, perhaps unwittingly, a part of the act, or the sales team, often building up mediocre performances into something superlative – and, often, failing to criticise when a player made a public exhibition of his bad temper.[1]

Packer's staff were largely business, not sports, people. Two years later, a compromise was reached between the ACB and Packer, and it was clear the board had made many concessions in terms of the international matches it would stage. The number of the more commercial, one-day matches taking place was dramatically increased.

On the positive side, Packer introduced to cricket a vitality and glamour it had previously lacked and introduced a whole new audience to the game who would otherwise have ignored its existence. This was encouraged by his introduction of 'pyjama cricket', one-day matches played under floodlights, using coloured clothing and with a white ball. He also brought the rewards of a cricket career more into line with the salaries of other professional sportspeople. Many players and staff outside the WSC fold soon found themselves with a 500 per cent pay increase.

But other aspects of Packer's commercialisation of cricket were less laudable. For one, the character of the game changed. Now that can be a good thing if a game is notably lacking in certain areas. But Packer turned his cricket from a slow-paced, subtle art to a fast-paced piece of showbiz, more reminiscent of American baseball. For this, many cricket fans and commentators feel he did a permanent disservice to the game. The slower style of spin bowling gave way to the onslaught of more aggressive, fast bowling, mainly because it would make better television. This was the stage at which many cricketers started wearing protective headgear, which would previously have been thought absurd by white-clad teams on village greens and by county players.

As so often happens when TV wants higher viewer ratings, a handful of personalities were glorified and bad behaviour dwelt on with relish. The Australian cricketer David Hookes was paid 5,000 Australian dollars to grow a beard and have it shaved in public by two models – the sort of antics previously associated more with pop idols than cricketers. In the 1982-3 season, Channel Nine presented their cricket 'Aggro Awards'. The British tabloid press and other media have followed suit with their obsessive reporting (or inventing) of the naughty goings-on in the life of Test Match cricketers, particularly when abroad. Ian Botham is in the same tabloid bracket as Joan Collins.

The TV cult of personality meant that more than ever, personalities were encouraged to stay on, even if technically they were past their best as players, because they drew the ratings. It has been claimed that this was at the expense of good cricket and of new blood entering the game.

By increasing the number of games played, it also put added pressure on players themselves. This has not been a problem confined to Australia. The Packer affair was a catalyst in the process which has seen commercial interests worldwide playing a bigger role in the structure of cricket. Because matches draw sponsorship money and TV ratings, more Test Matches are being played. Now a team may play up to fifteen a year, mostly overseas.

This is bad for the sport in two respects. Fans become jaded as a new Test Match is less of an event. In the long term interest may be lost in the pressure for immediate income. Secondly, players are overworked. In the past few years,

Ian Botham, David Gower, Graham Gooch and Mike Gatting – some of England's top players – have made themselves unavailable for winter tours. A major reason is their family life. For Gower, it was simply a matter of staleness. He had had too much sport, too much time spent away from home.

In the words of Graham Gooch: 'Your perspective changes when you've a young family... the more trips you've done the more your values change. In my case I feel I can never replace the years watching the kids grow up.'[2]

There is an additional pressure on the game which is caused by the search for ever larger television audiences. This is that it gives the wrong image of the game. Cricket as it was traditionally played was far from televisual. Now there is pressure to speed up the game to create more exitement. There is an illusion created by the showing of edited highlights that cricket is about hitting sixes, diving for stunning catches and arguing with umpires.

It is not. In fact, the essence of cricket is not good television – a medium which demands action and conflict to sustain interest. So cricket is made to fit the TV schedules, and not vice-versa. Simon Jones, author of *The Sunday Sport Question*, illustrates the point:

No one who witnessed it will forget the breathtaking finish to probably the closest Ashes Test Match in history at Melbourne in 1982. Channel Nine had covered the game throughout, and with four runs or one wicket to win, had slavishly gone over to the commercials, only to miss the decisive moment! It somehow encapsulated the triumph of commercialism.[3]

The effect was similar to that of watching moving drama on commercial TV. Two instances stick in my mind. One is of watching *Othello*, perhaps Shakespeare's most tense and agonizing tragedy, only to have the murder scene interrupted by three spivs dancing across the screen, advertising crisps. And the re-creation of the pivotal point of history, the crucifixion scene in *Jesus of Nazareth*, was punctuated by adverts for consumer durables.

Sport and Sponsorship

Sponsorship itself, many would say, has broadly been a good thing for sport. It has brought much-needed capital, and in turn has done a lot of good to the sponsors. Back in 1978 Cornhill were a minor insurance company with a public recognition of only two per cent. Five years later, as sponsors of English Test cricket, their name was known by 17 per cent of the public, and this had pushed them into the top division of insurance companies. Cornhill were happy and cricket was happy. Sponsorship is inseparable from sport. A randomly picked day's racing included the Gold Seal Oaks, the Air Hanson Handicap, the Multibroadcast Handicap, the Focus TV & Video Rental Handicap, the Philips Maiden Stakes and the Middlebrook Mushrooms Handicap.

However, there is a danger in sponsorship that the wares of the sponsors will be less suitable to the medium of sport. In fact, there is a built-in likelihood that companies unsuited to sport's healthy image will wish to associate themselves with it, in order to polish up their own public image. One example of this is Mars confectionery sponsoring fun-runs and marathons. In an age where people are turning against sugary sweets and chocolates for health reasons, the message of such sponsorship is that Mars not only helps you work, rest and play, it contributes to physical fitness and vitality.

But if sport holds appetising prospects for confectioners, how much more of an addiction does it hold for cigarette manufacturers. Money from the tobacco industry has become the life-blood of much sport in the UK and round the world. In 1986, a record £146 million was pumped into sport by cigarette companies. This compares with a figure of £16 million only ten years earlier. Hoardings around race tracks and stadia, logos on clothing, stickers on cars and on the side of boats, and even the colours and patterns on the cars, sing praises to brands of cigarette.

Of course, it is purely a way of advertising – an alternative to press adverts. And it is a way of advertising on television, where cigarette advertising on TV is not allowed. In 1965 ITV banned cigarette adverts, and the BBC has never allowed any advertising of any goods, in any form. But both channels cover sporting events.

Peter Taylor, in *The Smoke Ring*, points out the irony of the situation:

> In 1981, the BBC, which is not allowed to carry advertising, broadcast 72 hours of Embassy snooker, 36 hours of State Express snooker, 33 hours of John Player cricket, 20 hours of Benson & Hedges cricket, 12 hours of Benson & Hedges tennis, 12 hours of Benson & Hedges snooker, 11 hours of Benson & Hedges golf, 11 hours of Embassy darts, and nine hours of State Express golf.[4]

The irony did not go unnoticed by Central TV's *Spitting Image*:

> Now a look ahead to programmes on BBC1. At 7pm highlights of the Embassy World Snooker Championships, which is followed by cricket, including the Benson & Hedges Cup final and highlights of the Cornhill test. In Match of the Day, at 10.15pm, action from the Canon League and the Milk Cup fifth round replay. And finally, Profile: BBC Chairman Stuart Young explains why he will never allow advertising on the BBC.

Another irony lies in the fact that during the tabloid press scandal over England cricketer Ian Botham's alleged drug-taking, the very life-blood of cricket was nicotine.

Dr Frank Ledworth, Research Fellow in the Department of Education at Manchester University, carried out two experiments on 880 secondary schoolchildren to test whether tobacco-sponsored sport on TV had the same effect on them as a direct advertisement. His results, first published in the *Health Education Journal*, concluded:

> The case rests that sports sponsorship on BBC TV has been shown to act as cigarette advertising to children. There would thus appear to be good grounds for calling for the cessation of tobacco sports sponsorship on TV so as to prevent further circumvention of the laws banning the TV advertising of cigarettes.[5]

But the real irony is not that TV bans cigarette advertising and at the same time shows a massive amount of effective advertising. It is that sport, healthy and life-giving, should have been hijacked by tobacco, unhealthy and directly responsible for at least 50,000 premature deaths annually in the UK (according to Government figures; other estimates put it closer to 100,000). Few serious athletes smoke – it would impair their performance too much. But sport and tobacco have become all but inseparable.

The argument is advanced that without tobacco sponsorship sport would collapse. In some cases that may be true. It is only true because the tobacco companies have worked hard to make this the case. They have made themselves indispensable to sport. The sports industry has become addicted to tobacco. They can't contemplate giving up, despite all the health evidence, because of the withdrawal effects. It would cause discomfort, but if they hadn't got hooked in the first place, there would have been no need for withdrawal.

It is the situation of a smoker who longs to give up but fears the effects – the shaking hands, the nerves, the craving and so on. Yet all the time it is nicotine, the drug in the tobacco, which causes the shaking hands and craving. It makes itself indispensable and then parades itself as a calmer and rescuer, whilst all the time dealing not in life but death.

Sunday Sports

Another attempt to remould the character of sport in the

image of the consumer society came in 1987, in the form of a Private Member's Bill in Parliament, which its sponsor described as 'a harmless little bill'. The sponsor was Lord (Woodrow) Wyatt, chairman of the Horserace Totalisator Board (the Tote) – the sport's own betting authority. The Bill was the Sunday Sports Bill. This was followed soon after by a second, almost identical, bill, the Sunday Sports (No 2) Bill. This was sponsored by Conservative MP Nicholas Soames.

Both bills sought to legalise on-course betting after noon, off-course betting after noon, and admission by charge on the gate at all sporting events on Sundays. All three of these were (and still are) currently illegal, under the terms of the Betting Gaming and Lotteries Act 1963 and the Sunday Observance Act 1780. On the face of it, Lord Wyatt seemed to have an appealing case. An old, restrictive law ought to give way to modern needs, and for the future success of sport.

The foreseen effects of Lord Wyatt's Bill were that the total profits from betting would rise and that more people might go to sports events and race meetings if they were held on Sundays. Some events currently taking place on Saturdays might also move to Sundays. It would legalise many fixtures which were currently taking place illegally on a Sunday. Or, to be more accurate, these events are not taking place illegally, but it is illegal for money to be received at the gate of professional sports events on Sunday.

In reality, Lord Wyatt's nonchalance was a smokescreen for a Bill which would have a very profound effect not only on sport, but on the very character of life in Britain. A more accurate context for the Bill was provided, at the time it was being debated in Parliament, by Peter Corrigan of *The Observer*:

> Now sport has developed the commercial gleam in the eye that controls all other aspects of our life – and the thought of all those people wasting their time walking, playing or lolling about in the armchair when they could be spending money is no longer to be tolerated.[6]

So the motive of the Sunday Sports Bills was, ultimately, profits and not necessarily the best interests of the sport or of society at large. More money for the sport is not necessarily a good thing if something vital to the sport is lost in the process of getting that money. And in the case of Sunday sports, something certainly would be lost.

Sunday Sport – the Victims

One group to suffer from the proposed Bills would have been workers in the sports industry. The Bills contained no employee protection for those not willing to work on Sundays to cope with the extra work. According to the *Newmarket Weekly News*, 55 of the 60 stable lads at one of the stables in the heart of British horseracing were opposed to Sunday sport. They already worked six days a week, often six and a half, and for long hours. Sunday was the one day when the pace slackened and it was possible to recuperate. Sunday sport would certainly have meant a seven-day week. Many would have been forced to choose between, on the one hand, their love of horses and the racing business and, on the other, areas such as family life, time with friends and church life.

Betting shop staff opposed the bill – after all, who wanted to be given an ultimatum of going to work on the day which friends and family had off – or risk losing their job? Staff working at sports grounds, transport drivers associated with the sports world, police to keep an eye on fixtures – all these and more would have to work on their current day off. It was estimated that up to 40,000 more people would be drawn into Sunday work. The Transport and General Workers' Union, representing many of those who would be called on for Sunday work, announced at a London press conference that they were solidly opposed to the Sunday sport moves.

Even those who stood to profit and who had the financial

interests of the racing industry at heart were not all in favour. At the time the Bills were before Parliament, I interviewed Sir Mark Prestcott, a top Newmarket trainer, and asked him what he felt about the Bills. He told me that he could understand the financial logic – Sunday racing and betting would bring more money into the industry. However, he could not support the moves for a very simple reason – he valued his Sunday too much. Like the stable staff, it was his one day of rest, when the gallop of the week gave way to a slower trot.

Also affected would be those living near sports grounds. Their day of relative peace would be disturbed. Polls show the great majority of people value a day when the streets are quiet and they can recuperate from the week's activities and, as I point out in the next chapter, this is biologically necessary. How would this need square with the road outside filling up with cars, coaches and melodic soccer fans on your day off?

Sportsmen and women themselves would be adversely affected. Those involved in full-time and even amateur sport are starting to show signs of premature burn-out and stress resulting from congested fixtures and resulting under-performance. Now, more than ever, sports people need a day off.

Barrington Williams, former British Indoor Long Jump champion and sprinter at the Seoul Olympics, confirmed this when I spoke to him about Sunday sport: 'Athletes know that the body needs a rest in order to regain lost strength. For me, Sunday is my rest day. On this day I always feel spiritually and physically refreshed.'

This is echoed by David Sheppard, former England cricket captain and now Bishop of Liverpool:

I argued consistently against the introduction of regular, professional Sunday cricket. I always believed that private or semi-private enjoyment of sport was quite another matter from organized, commercial sport. I regret that we lost that argument and that professional cricketers and those whose regular work involves them with the game have no choice about how they spend Sunday. Together with the increase of overseas tours, this seven days a week cricket has much to answer for in the stress and sometimes break-up of marriages and family life.

An unstated factor, but one certainly present in the debate over Sunday professional sport and betting, is the wider issue of Sunday trading. If a horse race is taking place, then the betting shops will open. With betting shops open, it would be harder for Parliament to be logical and consistent in rejecting other Sunday trading. Sunday sport would act as a Trojan Horse to smuggle in consumerism into the Sunday High Street.

This would also result in an extraordinary situation. The Jockey Club, which fixes race meeting dates, would have power over commercial activity in the High Street! The character of your town would be determined in part by an unelected body – without any reference to local government or the local community.

Finally, the character of sport generally would suffer. The essence of sport lies in participation. It is about activity to make yourself healthier, about exertion, about getting out of the house, about meeting friends in a different context. Sunday is a key day for amateur sport. Because it is the one day most people are free from work it is also the day people are free to play football at the local recreation ground, go for a round of golf, play cricket on the village green. This keen amateur enthusiasm for sport has a long tradition in Britain.

Yehudi Menuhin wrote in his autobiography about his first memories of Britain, including 'Mr Alexander L. Howard, a wood merchant, whose knowledge of his subject went beyond the demands of commerce into delight in the thing itself. He was my first example of that amateurism, an elevated interest and pleasure in life, which I count among Britain's most admirable qualities.'[7]

This enthusiastic amateurism is particularly true of sport. But the sense of amateurism is under threat. Consumerism says that if something is worthy of fascination it is capable of making money. Everything has a price tag. The logic is simple: a spectator pays good money, an amateur player running around a field does not. Therefore we need to turn more players into spectators.

If professional sport takes over Sunday it would not only fill sports grounds around the country, it would also receive wide live TV coverage. As such, it would further detract from amateur sport on a day set aside for participation.

People would be on the terraces instead of the field, they would be in the armchair in front of the TV rather than kicking, batting or running. The 1964 Crathorne Committee, the most recent Government-appointed body to look at the pros and cons of professional Sunday sport, stated that the law restricting paid sport had encouraged the growth of participatory sports.

But, as so often happens, health and relationships are not included in the financial equation. Participation in sport is an important part of a healthy society. Widespread professional Sunday sport and betting would turn us even more into a nation of watchers rather than doers.

The increasing role played by the banknote in sport is particularly ironic since sport is one of the main areas of modern life which can help us restore a balance. Sport can remind us of those dimensions of life which consumerism tries to erase:

▷ It can build relationships and help us transcend individualism. Playing sport in a team forces us to consider others and play alongside others. Selfish individualists are rarely popular in a team. And the fun of throwing a frisbee together, playing squash, playing football in the street all draw us out of ourselves into a realm of shared fun and experience, and can deepen relationships.

▷ It can redirect the competitive drive. Competition is not bad in itself. But consumerism identifies competition with 'keeping up with the Joneses' and personal success at the expense of the next person. Sport asserts that competition is a pitting of one's wits and body against another person for mutual enjoyment. Consumerism locks us into a system of insatiable wants and dissatisfactions. Sport asserts that whatever your level, you can become a winner. Consumerism says a sense of achievement is always just around the corner, available at a price.

▷ Sport is a simple reminder in our everyday lives that the most fun parts of being human don't carry a price tag. In an age where shops, advertisers and moneylenders offer us paradise at a price, amateur sport can be an act of defiance which reminds us that the best things in life really are free.

The commercialisation of sport is a subtle twisting of sport away from relationships, health, leisure and keen amateurism, towards the cash register. And, as Simon Jones concludes: 'The Sunday sports initiative, if it does succeed, will not simply "clean up" the inconsistencies in the law and give it back the dignity of being respected. It will remove all there is to control the inexorable advance of sporting big business.'[8]

So who are the *real* spoilsports?

Notes

[1] Christopher Martin-Jenkins, *Twenty Years On* (Collins: London, 1984) p 107.

[2] Quoted in Simon Jones, *The Sunday Sport Question* (Jubilee Centre Publications: Cambridge, 1987).

[3] *Ibid.*

[4] Peter Taylor, *The Smoke Ring* (Sphere: London, 1984) p 104.

[5] *Health Education Journal* No 43 (4), 1984.

[6] Peter Corrigan, 'Sunday Bloody Sunday', *The Observer* 24

January, 1988.
[7] Yehudi Menuhin, *Unfinished Journey* (Futura: London 1978) p 163.
[8] Simon Jones, *op cit.*

6

SUNDAY – NOT FOR SALE

Consumerism Goes on the Offensive

'An Outdated Law'?

Question: When is a pair of stockings not a pair of stockings?
Answer: When it is a fan-belt.
Question: When is a roll of wallpaper not a roll of wallpaper?
Answer: When it is a car accessory.

These are not two surreal jokes invented by a bad humorist.
They are both claims made in a British court of law, just two
of the absurdities thrown up by the debate over Sunday trading.

The bizarre definitions were given by a judge as examples
of how certain stores were attempting to get round the law
governing what can and cannot legally be sold on a Sunday.
As it stands, the law does not allow for the sale of clothing or
decorating equipment. But it does make provision for
emergency car spares. A store had been accused of illegal
trading on a Sunday, and had defended itself by saying the
stockings it sold could be used as a spare fan-belt, and its

126

wallpaper to decorate a mobile home. Needless to say, the judge ruled that the store in question was bending the English language a little too far.

These are examples of how shops have tried to twist the law to suit their own ends. Other retailers have abandoned any attempt to stay within the law and flagrantly break it by opening illegally on Sunday.

So the argument has arisen: surely we should do away with such an outdated law. Certainly, this is the view put forward by the majority of the Conservative party, many large retailers and the greater part of the national press. And, at least superficially, their case for scrapping the Sunday trading law seems a strong one.

In 1986, during the debate over the Shops Bill to get rid of the law, the national press was full of features and editorials telling us that the law was old-fashioned and unsuited to modern life, that nobody wanted it, that you could buy a pornographic magazine on a Sunday but not a Bible, and that a fundamentalist religious minority were trying to force their views on society. Indeed, if your only source of news was the national press or Conservative Party press releases, you could be forgiven for thinking that there was no real opposition to this view, apart from a tiny group of loony Sabbatarians.

Believing all you read in the press can be a dangerous business. For the push for Sunday trade is a prime example of a con-trick played on the British public by a minority who would stand to make a profit from dumping a law inconvenient to themselves. It is an example of the consumer society going on the offensive and greedily gobbling up anything which threatens to stand in its way.

But to appreciate this, we need to look a little closer at each of the plausible-sounding justifications for commercialising Sunday which so many of us assume to be true because we hear them repeated so many times. We need to look closer at the myths of Sunday trading:

▷ The public wants it.

▷ Retailers want it.

▷ It will give the consumer greater freedom of choice.

▷ The current law is full of anomalies and is unenforceable.

▷ It will be good for the economy.

▷ It is an essential part of Conservative ideology.

▷ Our Sunday laws are more restrictive than those in Europe.

▷ Shopworkers wouldn't have to work if they didn't want to.

▷ Trading wouldn't greatly affect the character of Sunday.

▷ A religious fringe can't impose their views on the rest of society.

A fairly overwhelming case in favour of allowing Sunday shopping. Or is it?

The public wants it

The evidence used to back up this claim is from national opinion polls. In March 1988 a Mori Poll on Sunday trading commissioned by the National Consumer Council, and widely reported in the press, found that 62 per cent of those questioned were in favour of Sunday trading.

What was not reported was the unstated bias in the poll. When the public are asked a question phrased as an issue of freedom and personal benefit as opposed to restriction and loss, it is easy to predict in advance what the answer will be.

So simply to ask, 'Are you in favour of Sunday trading?' is a little like asking, 'Would you like to pay less tax?' It invites a positive answer. After all, who would admit to wanting to pay more tax? In a snap decision – which is what polls demand – the immediate inclination is to give the answer which seems to hold out the most immediate benefit for you. Human nature is such that people automatically jump for personal gain without considering the social and wider implications. Parliament, which had to balance the freedom of some against the accompanying hardship it would cause others, recognised in 1986 that social safeguards were essential if society was not to be a selfish free-for-all. They duly threw out the Bill to bring in Sunday trading.

If people were not asked simply, 'Would you like to pay less tax?' but, 'Would you like to pay less tax if it meant hospitals were understaffed, the mentally handicapped were not cared for and our nation was left undefended?' the response would be very different. That is no more a biased question than the earlier one. If you have a tax cut it will mean less money is available for public spending.

Similarly, if people were asked 'Would you like Sunday trading, if it meant you lost a day of rest, prices went up, your local shop went out of business, tension and stress in society increased, religious freedom was restricted and family and community life were damaged?' I suspect people might not be so keen to say yes! All of these are entirely justifiable forecasts of what would happen if Sunday trading was to be introduced.

Interestingly, this issue of how questions are phrased is borne out by a Poll in November 1985, carried out by the Co-operative Union. In it, 70 per cent agreed that 'it would be a shame if Sunday became just like any other day' and 75 per cent welcomed a day when their streets were quiet from the bustle of a weekday. A majority in favour of keeping Sunday a special day. Likewise, a major survey by *Woman* magazine of 13,000 of its readers on their shopping habits found that 64 per cent said a clear 'No' to Sunday trading. Only 11 per cent said they wanted it.

When the Oxford Street Association, representing the

traders of the large London shopping street, asked 2,300 shoppers whether they would like seven-day shopping if it meant they would have to pay more for goods (which the Association felt would be a likely consequence), four out of five said no.

The other fact about the 62 per cent supposedly in favour of Sunday trading in 1988 is that two years earlier, 69 per cent of the public had said yes to Sunday trading. So even with a biased survey, the percentage of people saying they wanted Sunday trading had fallen.

Public opinion has been misrepresented by the media and those with a vested interest in commercialising Sunday. There is no widespread consumer demand for it. When BBC Radio 4's *Call Nick Ross* programme debated Sunday trading, the switchboard received more than 4,000 calls from the public (the second highest ever for the programme) and two-thirds had been in favour of keeping Sunday special.

Gallup surveys in London's Oxford Street in both 1985 and 1987 showed that less than one per cent thought Sunday shopping would improve the shopping environment. Letters to Home Secretary Douglas Hurd on the subject of Sunday trading were running at 650-1 against the Government during the Shops Bill debate. A majority in favour of Sunday trading? Come off it!

Retailers want it

Obviously, a large number of retailers are in favour of Sunday trading: they are the ones putting millions of pounds behind the latest national publicity campaign to change public opinion in favour of a commercialised Sunday.

But it would be wrong to conclude that because a noisy few want it, most traders do. Most don't. The reason is that for most of them, it would be uneconomical.

Take, for example, a lawn-mower shop. If seven-day trading was introduced, the owner would have to pay more in salaries to shopworkers and cleaners, and there would be the added costs of heating and light. And, since he would be producing an extra day's waste paper and other rubbish, he would eventually have to pay his council more in rates: dustbin-men won't work for free. Nor will traffic wardens, police and everybody else drawn in to cope with the added work created.

So will you and I buy more lawn-mowers to cover these extra costs? Of course not! Grass will still grow at the same rate, Sunday trading won't create any more grass to be mown. It makes economic sense: either the shopkeeper will have to put his prices up, he will have to pay his staff less, or – eventually – he will go out of business because he can't cope with the lower profit-margins. None of them very attractive options for a shopkeeper.

Then, couldn't he simply remain closed on Sunday? Nobody is forcing him to open. It's not that simple. If his competitor is open on Sunday, he can't afford *not* to open as well. Otherwise, customers will go to the competitor and he will lose market-share. So, although he knows that in the long run, he and his competitor might lose out, he will have to open.

A useful analogy is that of a football match or music concert. If the person in front of you stands up, you have to stand up too, or else you won't be able to see. Then the person behind you stands up too. Soon everybody is standing up. Nobody has a better view than when they started – but they all start getting sore legs. Nobody really benefits.

What results is an absurd situation where the retailer is left with no choice: either open and lose out, or remain closed and lose out even more. Retailers won't be able to afford not to open if competitors are open. Most retailers are thankful for Sunday because they know all their competitors are also closed (except for a few lawbreakers – more of whom later). Everybody abides by the rules. If you do away with rules and create a free-for-all the whole game is spoilt.

For this reason, the list of retailers and retail groups solidly opposed to Sunday trading is a formidable one: John Lewis Partnership, C&A, Marks & Spencer, Co-op, National

Chamber of Trade, Alliance of Independent Retailers, British Hardware Federation, National Federation of Meat Traders, National Pharmaceutical Association, Drapers Chamber of Trade, Multiple Shoe Retailers Association, and countless others, including large multiples with commercial reasons for not wanting to be publicly identified with either side in the Sunday debate.

When the trade magazine *Retail Week* carried out a survey of retailers, in conjunction with computer giant ICL, it found that the majority did not want to open on Sunday, and that only 13 per cent said they would be prepared to invest in a campaign. It also found that 78 per cent of independent DIY stores are against Sunday trading.[1]

The real pressure for Sunday trade comes, then, not from the majority of traders but from a minority who see themselves as taking a sizeable market share from smaller traders if Sunday trading comes in. These are mainly the large, out-of-town DIY stores. An editorial in the November 87 edition of *DIY Superstore* magazine commented:

> It's absolutely crucial for the industry that this time a revised Shops Bill goes through without silly mistakes. After all, saturation point is fast approaching and superstores will need Sunday trading like never before.

One of the largest DIY chains, B&Q, have appointed a full-time Controller for Sunday Trading – somebody to work for deregulation. During the shops Bill one DIY chain was advertising that it would donate a penny to charity for every person who went to their store when they opened (illegally) on Sunday.

Because some of the DIY chains feel they can't wait for the law to be changed, they have chosen to deliberately break the law by opening anyway. Their resulting argument that we ought to scrap the law because it is unenforceable is like saying the law of manslaughter is unenforceable because people kill people! Surely, the correct conclusion is that we ought to enforce the law more strongly, rather than get rid of it.

The comparison is not so silly. By opening illegally, the large DIYs are performing a criminal act – they are unfairly gaining a trading advantage over other shops who refuse to open illegally. It would be sheer hypocrisy for a lawbreaking DIY to call for the enforcement of the law on shoplifting while they choose to ignore the law safeguarding Sunday. Despite complaints from other traders and from the shopworkers' union, USDAW, the lawbreaking continues because they are frequently not prosecuted. The average weekly sum set aside by Councils to enforce the law is a paltry £27.

Even if the stores are prosecuted, many simply pay the fine and carry on illegal trading because it is still profitable to do so. It is not so much that the law is at fault as that some big stores deliberately choose to break it because it is not convenient to them, and that some councils and even the Government turn a blind eye to the lawbreaking.

A feature in *Marketing* magazine commented:

> The Government, as it so often likes to tell the country, is the party of law and order. How, then, can it explain its position on Sunday trading? Up and down the country shops open for business on Sundays in contravention of the 1950 Shops Act and yet the Conservative Party appears to turn a blind eye.[2]

This is something which angers Jonathan Swift, Managing Director of the British Hardware Federation, representing 5,000 independent DIY retailers, many of whom are being squeezed out of business by the lawbreakers. He said that large multiples could afford to break the law while his members could not:

> We aren't discussing whether the law should be changed to allow retailing on Sunday. We just want the existing law enforced. How can the Conservative Party claim it wants to help the self-employed when small family businesses are closing down because of its inaction?[3]

Even Margaret Thatcher told the House of Commons, in reply to a question about the enforcement of the Sunday trading laws: 'The law should be obeyed until changed by Parliament.'[4]

But the lawbreaking continues, as Government and Councils turn a blind eye to breaches of a law because many of them find it personally inconvenient.

The consumer society has generated a new style of crime. It is a High Street hooliganism where the criminals are not yobs in boots with shaven heads picking on smaller boys, but large multiple stores, living outside the law, who flex their financial muscles and force the smaller boys out of business.

It will give the consumer greater freedom of choice

To start with, consumers will have greater choice to shop because they will be able to choose to shop on Sunday.

But there the freedom of choice argument stops. As smaller stores are squeezed out of business because of the added overheads of seven-day opening, the freedom of where you can shop will gradually diminish. Particularly at risk will be the small, local stores, frequently used by the elderly and less mobile. Freedom of choice for the mobile and able-bodied will mean a reduction of freedom for the less advantaged. Also, it is unlikely that a full public transport system – such as buses – would operate on Sundays, so people who rely on this form of transport, particularly the less well off and the elderly, would be further penalised.

If any prices rise as a result of Sunday trading, consumers will be denied freedom to buy goods at the lowest possible price. When the pub opening hours were deregulated in 1988 the prices of drinks went up in some pubs by as much as 8p each. The reason given was that it was to cover the cost of the longer opening hours. Freedom of choice not to open will be taken away from the shopkeepers. Freedom of choice to have a day when the streets are relatively quiet and empty will be taken away from residents.

Freedom of choice to spend time with family and friends will be denied to many shopworkers. Freedom of choice to have Sunday lunch with the family (as 82 per cent of the population choose to do at the moment, according to a June 1988 Marplan Poll) would be denied. Freedom of churches to hold services when everybody can be present because they have a day off will be denied.

Freedom of choice even to shop on Sunday will be progressively removed from an increasing percentage of the public as the 'ripple effect' of Sunday work spreads and more and more people are drawn into seeing Sunday as just another work day: those who clean or police the streets, regulate or drive public transport, and so on.

Dr Kirby of the University of Wales reported to the Auld Committee, set up to examine the potential effects of Sunday trading:

> The increased decline of the independent sector would be damaging to the interests of the manufacturers and suppliers who, increasingly, would become dependent on the large retail organisations as outlets for their products.[5]

So what choice for the manufacturers and suppliers?

Clearly, 'freedom' is an ambiguous term. One person's freedom can mean another's slavery. And, anyway, even the freedom of choice for consumers argument is suspect. Why should they be able to pursue their freedom at the expense of the rest of society, particularly the less privileged? An editorial in *The Daily Mirror* (15 August 1988) says of Sunday trading:

> It may not be what church leaders, or shop assistants or some trade unions want. But it's what the customers want. And they're the ones who matter.

This claim is outrageous for several reasons. One is the idea that a customer somehow matters more than a shopworker

because the customer is the one with money. It says that consumption is a higher, nobler goal than justice (and that from a
supposedly left-wing newspaper!) And it tells shopworkers –
who are also consumers themselves – that they are only valuable in their capacity as consumer, that as a worker or family
member or member of a community they deserve no rights.
What was I saying in chapter two about identifying people by
consumer means, and how this can squeeze out other roots of
identity?

A society (or political ideology) which can only understand
freedom of choice in terms of supermarket shelves is morally
sick.

The current law is full of anomalies and is unenforceable

The most common example of an anomaly in the existing law
is that you can't buy a Bible on a Sunday but you can buy a
pornographic magazine. This is because books cannot be
sold, whereas periodicals and newspapers can, since they are
on Schedule Five of the 1950 Shops Act, the list of goods
exempted from the law.

But does this cause real hardship? I would doubt if many
shop assistants receive a mouthful of abuse from a shopper
who, having just bought his dirty magazine, is angry because
he is denied a Bible. This 'anomaly' is more a debating-point
than a hardship. In a sense, even this anomaly has a sensible
basis. To open all bookstores nationwide would have a
dramatic effect on the feel of the day, not to mention the
economic and social repercussions. But newsagents have to
be open for at least part of Sunday so people can buy their
Sunday papers.

A deeper point is at stake. Does the existence of anomalies
in itself discredit a law? The answer has to be no. The VAT
laws, for example, contain similar anomalies. A hot pie qual-
ifies for VAT, whereas a cold pie does not. Few laws are perfectly tidy. The point at issue is whether a few anomalies
invalidate a law designed to prevent a greater social evil. In

the case of the Sunday laws, the answer has to be no. The idea of a general ban on Sunday commercialism, with the exception of a few exempted goods, such as food provisions, emergency car spares and newspapers is remarkably sensible.

As we noted above, the law is not unenforceable. It is simply that certain shops choose to flout the law and certain councils choose not to enforce it. Admittedly, the law may need a little updating to bring it into line with changes in retailing since it was originally formulated, but that is quite a different matter. A law such as that of Germany, Italy and the Netherlands might be a satisfactory way to update the law. These countries restrict opening but have a list of exempt shops (not goods) which are allowed to open.

It will be good for the economy

Research shows that total sales in the retail sector would rise only slightly, if at all. So, even if we thought a 'grow, grow, grow' economy was desirable, Sunday trading would not help us realise it.

When the Auld Committee was set up by the Government to look into the possible effects of Sunday trading, the Committee invited the Institute of Fiscal Studies to give an economic forecast. The IFS reported that if, over a fifteen-year period, sales remained more or less static, then up to 20,000 full-time equivalent jobs could actually be *lost* through Sunday trading.

The only substantial rise in sales is likely to go to some big DIYs and garden centres – hence the lawbreaking and all the fuss from their corner about scrapping the law. But their profits will be gained at the expense of smaller stores and a wider cost in social terms. It is these arguments we shall look at later.

It is an essential part of Conservative ideology

Conservatives who want to see Sunday kept special are made to feel they are being unfaithful to the party's ideals and to free-market economic policies. Hardly an argument which will have any persuasive power if you are a socialist or a 'green', but this can create a real dilemma of conscience to a committed Conservative who nevertheless feels that Sunday trading is wrong. But the tension need not exist.

Many of the great and respected Conservatives of the recent past were ardent supporters of Sunday as a day of rest. One of these was Lord Stockton, the former Conservative Prime Minister Harold Macmillan. On 21 January 1986 he told the House of Lords:

> Let us remember that the great commandment that was handed down to God's chosen people was perhaps the greatest social reform in the history of civilisation: the concept that every man or woman, however humble, should have at least some period of rest.

Indeed, the greatest Conservative Prime Minister of this century, Winston Churchill, believed Sunday should be kept special. In *The Daily Telegraph* of 27 December 1933, he explained why. It is worth quoting from the article since the arguments are all still relevant:

> There is need of immediate action in respect to the growing evil of Sunday trading.... (Sunday) is the necessary pause in the national life and activity; it is essentially the day of emancipation from the compulsion and strain of daily work; it is the birthright of every British subject, a day of personal, social and spiritual opportunities, and, above all, our great heritage, and one it is our duty to hand on to posterity unsullied by the commercialisation which is making its mark today...
>
> The rising flood of Sunday trading, which results in forcing thousands to work against their inclination, must be stemmed.

The former leader of the Conservative grouping in the European Parliament, Sir Fred Catherwood, is a patron of the Cambridge-based Keep Sunday Special Campaign.

Some of the most senior campaigners against Sunday trading today are also keen Conservatives. The Chairman of the Keep Sunday Special Campaign is Viscount Brentford, a Conservative peer in the House of Lords. The Campaign's Operations Director – in charge of day-to-day campaigning – is David Blackmore, a Conservative and former member of Colchester City Council. Various groups within the Conservative Party, such as the Conservative Family Campaign, also oppose moves to bring in Sunday trading. I even have a copy of a letter written by a certain Margaret Thatcher, would-be MP for Finchley back in 1970, in which she reassured a constituent:

> Thank you for your letter. My position does indeed remain as previously reported. I am very much against work, racing and gambling on Sundays.

At the time of the Shops Bill vote, no less than 72 Conservative MPs rebelled against a Three-Line Whip (a kind of parliamentary gun to the head to ensure MPs vote with the party line), and voted with the opposition parties against the Shops Bill. In so doing they ensured the Bill was defeated and Mrs Thatcher suffered her only major defeat in office. Clearly, such a large crowd of MPs would not risk embarrassing their Party in this way unless they felt it was a matter of key importance.

The issue at stake is the ideological split within the Tory Party. One group is the old, 'One Nation' school of Conservatism, exemplified by such Tories as Churchill and Macmillan. This school puts the stress on 'conserving' that which it sees as valuable in society. It is slow to welcome drastic change and sees a key role for the state in helping the less privileged. These value Sunday for its role in Britain's heritage (to use Churchill's word) – including its spiritual heritage – and its role in protecting groups such as shopworkers and the family.

The other school of thought is the more hard-line, free-market school, currently known as Thatcherism. It is this school of thought which dominates the Party today, and which is pushing for unrestricted Sunday trade. This group is against anything which it sees as putting limits on the ideal of completely free, unlimited trading. An uncommercialised Sunday seems to be a perfect example of such a limit.

However, the equation of Sunday trade with free markets has been questioned from within the Party. In a paper entitled *The Free Market and Public Safeguards*, the Conservative author Martin B. Graham argues that the free-market argument is simply not relevant to Sunday trading, since free-market arguments apply only to *how* markets operate, not *when*:

> If the market doesn't trade at all on Sundays considerations about *how* it should trade hardly seem to apply. Whether the market trades six or seven days a week is quite separate from the question if how it trades, when it does so. And the issues of competition and efficiency concern the manner, not the duration of trading.
>
> We are not worried, from the point of view of efficiency, that trading ceases at night. Nor should we be worried about its doing so on Sundays. All that matters in relation to efficiency is that when trading takes place, it does so in the manner of a free market, ie with open competition.[6]

Graham points out that in fact Sunday trading will make markets *less* efficient because of all the extra overheads. And when this is added to the social cost of seven-day working, he concludes that certain rules and limits are not only desirable but essential:

> Is it not appropriate, in all respects, that we drive on (say) the left and respect traffic signals at crossroads? And, in passing, is it not vastly more *efficient* that we should do so – that we should accept regulation – rather than shunning rules and supposing that a system of 'free competition' is in every instance more productive?[7]

Our Sunday laws are more restrictive than those in Europe

Some advocates of Sunday trading refer to the 'Continental

Sunday', supposedly a day of fun and freedom – unlike the grim limitations of the British Sunday.

But is this the case? If we look at the laws relating to Sunday trade, we find that practically all the countries of Europe have restrictions very similar, and in some cases virtually identical to those in the UK. In fact, in Germany there is a general push to *tighten up* the Sunday laws. Even the German conservatives, the Christian Democrats, are entirely happy that the special character of Sunday should be preserved. According to Christian Democrat Member of the European Parliament, Elmar Brok:

> In Germany our view is that Sundays should be kept special to preserve family life, and that opening shops on Sundays will lead to higher prices for the consumer.[8]

Simon Jones, author of the research document, *Evidence on the European Sunday*, concludes:

> In essence, the continental Sunday of unlimited shopping is a myth. In each country surveyed (all our major EEC partners), through one means or another, restrictions are placed on Sunday shopping. In West Germany and Holland the legislation is more stringent. Nowhere is it noticeably more liberal. A high premium is placed on keeping Sunday a different day.[9]

Members of the European Parliament – from right-wing German conservatives to Italian Communists – agree that Sunday trading has to be restricted. If Britain wishes to harmonise its laws with Europe, in view of the coming closer trade links, then the last thing we should do is change our Sunday laws. If we did, we really would be out of step with Europe.

Let's be more 'Mediterranean' about Sunday if we have made it too much of a grey, depressing day – let's make it a day for processions and parties. But there is no need to usher in a commercial free-for-all too. It is a sad reflection on society and us as individuals if we can only think of having fun in terms of cash and shopping trolleys.

Shopworkers wouldn't have to work if they didn't want to

When the Shops Bill was being debated in 1986 it did contain a clause about shopworker protection. But this aimed to protect only *existing* workers against unfair dismissal. It gave no protection for people who subsequently changed jobs or were given promotion.

Nor did it protect those starting work or the self-employed shopkeepers who would be forced to stay open so as not to lose market share. And even the few who are protected would be in an unenviable position. If you refused to work on Sunday because of family, church or other commitments – or on grounds of conscience – you would hardly be in the line for promotion. You would be inviting a label of awk-ward or unenthusiastic and inviting somebody else to take your place.

Shopworkers are the section of society who would be worst hit by Sunday trading. For this reason, some of the most dedicated campaigners for keeping Sunday special are the shop-workers' union, USDAW. According to the Union's Deputy General Secretary, John Flood, a 'conscience clause' is simply a red herring to get total deregulation through. He described the current Shops Act, which restricts Sunday trading, as 'the last bastion of protection for shopworkers'.

Of the 2.3 million shopworkers in British retailing (around a tenth of the total workforce in the UK), around half are mar-ried women. The effects of Sunday trading on their family life would be shattering. No more day spent at home with the fam-ily, no more day to travel to visit Granny and the wider family. An alternative day off – say a Wednesday – would be no com-pensation. On a Wednesday kids would be at school and a husband at work.

If Sunday was deregulated it would mean the end of 'pre-mium' (or 'unsocial hours') payments for working on a day set aside for family and leisure. Why should employers pay extra for Sunday work if Sunday was just another work day? One major High Street store is already employing part-timers for sixteen hours at weekends – at a Sunday rate exactly the same as a normal weekly rate.

It is a clear case of shopworkers, already a notoriously low-paid group, being singled out for unfair treatment and exploitation. The owner of a Barnstaple hardware store wrote to the trade magazine *Hardware Trade Journal*:

> The National Consumer Council MORI poll indicates that the majority of the general public want a free-for-all on the Sunday opening of shops.
>
> If those same people were asked if they would like doctors' and dentists' surgeries, civic centres and county halls, banks and post offices, coal mines and the offices of the National Consumer Council open on Sundays the reply would be the same. Has the consumer council put these questions to the 'consumer'? If not, why not?
>
> The answer is obvious. They know there is no other way any other workers would give way to this exploitation. It would be unthinkable for any individual county hall or bank or school to open as they please and require their workers to work throughout weekends. Why then single out the already exploited shopworker for this treatment?[10]

Some new shopping centres already make employees sign a contract which includes a clause promising to work on Sundays if the law were to be changed. So much for freedom to choose to say no. If you are in any doubt about how shopworkers feel about Sunday trading – go and ask one. In the words of USDAW's John Flood: 'USDAW is against Sunday trading purely because we think, as indeed millions of people in this country think, it's unnecessary and is not catering for the needs of a consumer society but for the greedy in a consumer society. The shopworkers, highly vulnerable and easily exploited – these are the people who will suffer and a conscience clause will not protect them.'

It wouldn't greatly affect the character of Sunday

Perhaps this is the greatest myth of all, used by pro-deregulation lobbyists to persuade the wavering. But Sunday trading *would* affect the day profoundly. As our lazy Sunday afternoon becomes just another manic Monday, the whole rhythm of life – including a day of rest – would be eroded.

Biologically, our bodies need a day of rest. In order to cope with the pressure of weekday life, our bodies raise the levels of adrenaline, noradrenaline and cortisol, our so-called stress hormones. The hormones increase our heart-rate and our rate of breathing and send bursts of energy to our muscles. The consequences of this are explained by Celia Wright in *Living* magazine:

> Everyone is familar with the unpleasant aspects of this response: the tension, the fear, the butterflies in the stomach.
>
> Less obvious are the *pleasurable* side effects. Cortisol, for example, has remarkable properties, suppressing pain, fatigue and allergic reactions and making us excited to the point of euphoria. In other words, it has all the hallmarks of an addictive drug.[11]

When our stress-hormone levels fall to their lowest level on Sundays, the day of rest, our body reminds us of the tiredness, illness, depression or pain we may have been suppressing during the week. It reminds us that we need a rest, otherwise we fall victim in the longer term to the stress-related illnesses of our consumer society.

Celia Wright concludes:

> The best way to break the hold of stress hormones over our lives is to award ourselves regular rest days in which we positively encourage those hormone levels to fall and so allow our bodies to recover from their effects... Sunday is traditionally the ideal rest day because most offices and shops are closed, partners are at hand to share domestic responsibilities, and the whole of British

life is geared to a slower pace.[12]

The results of seven-day commercialism would be an increase in stress and tension. There would no longer be a day when the streets are quiet, a day when we can temporarily opt out of the rat-race, a day when we can put work pressures and the lemming-like rush of consumerism on one side.

The Rev Dr Donald English, Secretary of the Methodist Church Home Mission Division, said Sunday 'establishes a kind of pattern for daily life which is intended for all humanity whether Christian or non-Christian: that we should have times when we're working and times when we have a break for recreation. One of the sad things about life today is that we are losing that sense. The hills and valleys are going and everything is becoming very flat.'

This is borne out by the report of the Government-appointed Auld Commission into Sunday trading, which states:

> Widespread opening of shops on Sunday would affect the traditional character of the day very much [more] profoundly than the opening of cinemas, concert halls and theatres, or the holding of sporting events. The change... would have a significant effect on the feel of the day. (Para 32).

Critics claim that the Scottish experience of Sunday trading proves that the character of the day wouldn't be changed. But the Government's own report, the Auld Report, said that Scotland cannot be used as a reliable indicator of what would happen in the rest of Britain. Scotland has a different population density, levels of car ownership, historical traditions and church commitment.

The reason that Scottish branches of many major stores do not currently choose to open is given by Archbishop Winning of Glasgow. Many Scottish stores choose not to open because they do not open in the rest of the UK:

Many of the big supermarkets have their branches here in Scotland but their headquarters are in England, and if the decisions were made there then it would be very, very unlikely indeed that their branches in Scotland wouldn't open as well. And there is really no great demand for it here.

Scotland proves nothing.

A religious minority can't impose their views on the rest of society

The first assumption of this frequently repeated bit of muddled thinking which needs to be knocked on the head is this: that most Christians want Sunday trading stopped because of Sabbatarian reasons – in other words, Sunday is the Sabbath and it is part of our religious observance to keep it holy, as the Jews were commanded to keep their Sabbath holy.

This is not the teaching of the church. Certainly, some Christians do see Sunday as the Sabbath, but it is no part of orthodox doctrine to do so. As Theodore Epp, in his small booklet, *The Sabbath or the Lord's Day?* bluntly puts it:

> Which day, then, is the Sabbath? Saturday of course. There is no such thing as a Christian Sabbath... What day, then, should the Christian set aside? There is no commandment given to Christians in this area. Every day of the week belongs to God.[13]

However, Epp points out that, historically, Sunday was the day Christ rose from the dead and the day on which he chose to meet with the disciples after his resurrection (note, he chose not to do this on a Sabbath but on a work day). Therefore Christians are justified in keeping Sunday as the Lord's Day. Not a day of duty, obligation and guilt, but a day which we gladly set aside to focus on God and others in a way which is impossible for the other six days in our busy lives.

As a Christian I find offensive the idea that God can be constrained into a 'Sunday best' box, that it is somehow worse to sin on a Sunday, that worship is a one-day-a-week activity, or that Sunday is holier than the rest of the week. These things smack more of folk-religion and superstition than Christian faith. If God is God of anything then he has to be God of everything – every day of the week, every human activity such as eating, reading, working, philosophising, sleeping and watching TV.

However, as a Christian, I am also glad that there is a day when, for practical reasons, I can meet together with fellow-believers in the knowledge that friends are there and not working in Marks & Spencer, operating cinema equipment or supervising a DIY store. I am glad that fellowship can be a reality because people are not prevented from coming together.

Seven-day working would remove the freedom of people to meet to worship on a shared day off. As such it would be a serious blow to religious freedom in a would-be tolerant state.

And as a Christian who believes the gospel speaks out against injustice, oppression and exploitation of the weak and stands up for family and community life, I have no choice but to oppose Sunday trading.

It is true, Christians do not have the right to impose their will on a largely secular society. But they have as much right as any other group to stand up for the sort of society they would like to see and to present well-reasoned arguments for it.

Britain has chosen to keep Sunday a special day since the time of King Athelstan (925–941). Everybody knows it's a different day from the other six. In opposing Sunday trading Christians are speaking not only on behalf of the churches, but also family and community life, retailers, shopworkers, the disadvantaged and the sanity of society as a whole.

The rapacious grasp of consumerism has to be told that there are some areas it cannot touch, islands of peace in a turbulent sea of materialism. Keeping Sunday special is a statement at national level that life is guided by other values than the purely commercial.

Notes

1. 'Thumbs down to Sunday Trade', *Retail Week* (17 June, 1988) p 1.
2. 'Shop Law Open to Debate', *Marketing* (17 December, 1988) p 13.
3. *Ibid.*
4. House of Commons, 11 December 1984.
5. Home Office, *Report of the Committee of Inquiry into Proposals to Amend the Shops Act*, Chairman Robin Auld QC (HMSO, 1984).
6. Martin Graham, *The Free Market and Public Safeguards* (Unpublished: Cambridge, 1988).
7. *Ibid.*
8. Quoted in Simon Jones, *Evidence on the European Sunday* (Jubilee Centre Publications: Cambridge, 1988).
9. *Ibid.*
10. *Hardware Trade Journal* 18 March 1988 p 42.
11. Celia Wright, 'Make Sunday Your Day of Rest' *Living* (February 1987) p 108.
12. *Ibid.*
13. Theodore H. Epp, *The Sabbath or the Lord's Day?* (Back to the Bible Books: Nebraska, 1958) p 16.

7

THE GLOBAL DUSTBIN

Consumerism and the Environment

Fouling the Nest

The holiday souvenir which has lasted me longest is not a toy donkey with salt and pepper on its back, a T-shirt or a piece of pottery. It is a large gloop of Mediterranean oil on my swimming trunks. Every time I swim it reminds me of my vacation on the sunny shores of the world's most polluted sea.

The main road near my house perennially blossoms plastic bags, tin cans, sweet wrappers and the Kentucky Fried Chicken packets which the public buy at a shop five miles away. They seem to wait till they approach my drive, throw out all the wrappers at once, and drive off chuckling into the night. Other people actually bring whole bags of rubbish out to the area of the Cambridgeshire countryside I live in and unload it all at the side of the road.

The problem of pollution is not simply one of aesthetics – although some of us persist in the old-fashioned notion that hedges do look better without the plastic and gaudy packaging. It is a matter of the very survival of the planet.

Like the problem of consumer debt, the scale of modern pollution is not a problem which has always been with us. It is a problem caused in large part by our consumer society. The Acropolis at Athens has suffered more structural damage in the last 20 years, as a result of environmental pollution, than it had in the previous 2,000. Our cities have become refuse tips which leak toxic wastes into the earth, our lakes and rivers are dying. Many of our trees and forest areas are dead already.

One reason for the pollution is the sheer quantity of waste which citizens of the consumer culture are producing. According to the World Conservation Strategy, produced by the Swiss-based International Union for Conservation of Nature and Natural resources, one Swiss person consumes the same amount of food, goods and raw materials as 40 Somalis. Similar figures could be quoted for the UK and North America.[1]

The Throw-Away Mentality

We live in a throw-away society. Tin cans have come a long way since the 1824 Arctic expedition, when a tin can was carried which bore the instructions: 'Roasted veal, cut round on the top near to the outer edge with a chisel and hammer.' Now the average family throws away twelve cans per week. 'Instant' and 'convenient' have been the order of the day since the 1950s. Food can be consumed instantly and the wrappers thrown away instantly. Less thought is given to what happens to all those wrappers. Each day the average American produces 4 kg (9 lbs) of hazardous waste. In the UK, according to Friends of the Earth, the figure is around 6 lb. Much of this is packaging, which accounts for about 10 per cent of our shopping bill.

The UK throws away 7 million tons of packaging each year. Much of this was never strictly necessary in the first place. Its job was to entice us to buy, to make the product appear more attractive as it jostles for space on crowded supermarket shelves, or to make unglamorous contents look exciting. An example of wasteful packaging sometimes quoted by environmental groups is the razor blade. The whole package is mounted on a laminated card. On this is a clear plastic bubble. This contains a white plastic container, which contains a printed card bearing the manufacturer's name, and waxed paper wrappers – which finally contain the blades. Then there is another piece of card, telling you not to forget to buy more blades. This is not to mention the paper bag which it may be put in (which you will also throw away), and a plastic carrier bag.

Another new element of the pollution problem is the kind of materials we are throwing away. Not only are we chucking out more and more, the objects of the chucking are more permanent. Unlike paper and wood, plastic does not naturally break down in the earth. It lasts for ever. A dead whale was found to have choked on 50 plastic bags. Mr and Mrs Average and their offspring throw out 90 lb of plastics every year. A welcome innovation has been biodegradable plastics, which return to nature when buried in the ground. Stores pioneering the use of the new, environment-friendly plastic bags include the Body Shop, Traidcraft and many wholefood shops. But the majority of stores still seem intent on leaving their logo for posterity on massive quantities of disposed-of plastic.

Bottles and Bottle-Banks

The issue of permanent waste can be seen particularly clearly in the case of glass bottles. Over 80 per cent of Britain's six billion bottles used each year are thrown away after just one use. This not only leaves permanent waste in the ground, it means the glass companies carry on using more and more of the earth's raw materials, when they could be reclaiming the perfectly reusable glass currently being thrown away. Enter bottle-banks. The banks were introduced in Britain as recently as 1977, by the Glass Manufacturers' Federation. The banks are large containers, usually situated in car parks in cities and large towns. The public bring their empties and leave them in the appropriate container – green, clear or coloured.

The manufacturers say the scheme saves them an annual energy equivalent of around five million gallons of oil in glass production. That is a 'lotta bottle', and constitutes a major contribution to care for the environment, but still lags way behind some other countries. In Holland, around 40 per cent of glass bottles are collected in 'bottle bins', found in most high streets. It is up to each of us to understand that care for the environment is not simply the hobby-horse of bearded eco-nuts (as the media sometimes – unkindly – portrays the ecologically concerned), but an issue which affects the quality of life on earth, and even its very future.

Yet bottle-banks are still only a second best in terms of care for the environment. Much more energy-efficient is reusing bottles, as currently happens with milk bottles in the UK. It isn't so long since most pop bottles had a deposit payable, repaid to you when you returned the bottle to the shop. That way you only paid for the contents. On shopping trips today it is increasingly hard to find any returnable bottles. Perhaps this owes a lot to our desire for convenience and lack of hassle. But we have to understand that it is we who pay for the glass. The bottle cost is included in the price of the drink. There is also the cost to the environment as holes in the ground rapidly fill up with once-used containers and young children at the beach paddle through the glassy sea – and cut their feet.

But there is no reason why we should not encourage the use of returnable bottles. Nine US states have banned non-returnable bottles. Oregon, the first of these, introduced the law to reduce the litter in its countryside and to cut down on the quantity of broken glass on its beaches. Now over 90 per

cent of bottles are reused. The total quantity of rubbish produced by the people of Oregon has fallen by 40 per cent since
the law was introduced. New York State followed suit in 1983.

Recycling expert and Oxfam worker Jon Vogler says it was
no coincidence that it was the glass manufacturers who
pioneered bottle banks. With the threat of more states and
nations introducing mandatory reusing of bottles, they
foresaw less work for their industry and panicked:

> Oregon, the 'Green State', might be dismissed as cranky but not
> New York. There was alarm in the bottle makers' boardrooms.
> Returnables might create jobs but reduced demand would
> puncture the ballooning profits of the glass industry.[3]

Vogler's conclusion is that while bottle banks may help con-
serve resources and lead to a tidier environment, they are not
the final answer. That lies in a change of attitude from being
a disposing society to a conserving society:

> One thing is certain, the government needs to respond to the
> EEC with a genuine policy of sorting and reusing beverage con-
> tainers to save energy, conserve materials, reduce dumping and
> create jobs. And for that matter so does every other affluent
> nation in our polluted and energy-profligate world.[4]

Obsolescence

But the consumer society understands terms such as 'con-
serve' and 're-use' less well than 'disposable' and 'obsolescence'. Obsolescence – the process of goods becoming obsolete and unusable – is a hallmark of consumerism.

There are three main types of obsolescence. They are of
function, quality and desirability.

Obsolescence of function

This is the most acceptable form of obsolescence. It occurs when a product is superseded by a superior product. Wax audio cylinders were replaced by LP records, which are in turn being replaced by compact discs. At each stage the improvement in the quality of sound reproduction makes the earlier form less desirable and hence obsolete. Black and white TVs are superseded by colour. Old, heavy walking boots which leave the walker with blisters by the newer, lighter models, old aeroplanes by newer models.

Of course, we need to be careful. Some people have the odd belief that just because something is new it must be better. This can be debatable: nuclear power is not necessarily more desirable than windmills, new foods are not necessarily better for you than traditional fare, new philosophies and theologies don't necessarily answer human need better than a system from centuries ago.

But the point remains. When a product is invented which performs the function better, with no more adverse side-effects than the item it replaces, obsolescence of function is a good thing.

Obsolescence of quality

This is what is commonly known as 'built-in obsolescence'. It means that after a certain, limited time, the product self-destructs or wears out. The effect of this is to ensure that people keep on buying products, to keep on generating more profits, and to 'keep the economy strong'. If the point of life is to generate more goods and more profits, permanence and durability of goods can be a sin.

I clearly remember as a small child going with my mother as she returned some badly made shoes to the shop. When she complained that they had lasted only a few months, the manager of the shop expressed his amazement that she should want shoes which lasted more than six months. Shoes which fall apart, he said, were good because they gave you the opportunity to go out and choose some more shoes sooner.

Many is the Christmas when I have watched children play excitedly with toys they had spent Advent lusting after on TV advertisements, only to find them broken by Boxing Day. My mother-in-law recently bought a pair of trousers which came unstitched after only a few days. You could add more examples from your own experience.

The existence of groups such as the Consumer Association, publishers of *Which?* magazine have done much to ensure that 'death-dating' is less prominent than it was when Vance Packard published his book *The Waste Makers* in 1960. Packard quotes several instances of deliberate introduction of obsolescence in the 1950s: the lifespan of the electric light bulb, home furnishing, portable radios, engineering. But the reasons for Packard's basic unease remain: that in a consumer society the production of junk – quickly used, quickly disposed of – is a positive virtue. Things may have improved a little since Packard's warnings, but we are still a long way from having a faith in quality, craftsmanship and durability. Until we do, they'll keep on producing the junk, and our dustbin which we call the Earth will keep being filled with it.

Obsolescence of desirability

Less obvious is a different sort of obsolescence, that of desirability. If the consumer doesn't even want the product after six months, he feels he only has him or herself to blame. The manufacturer is seen not as con-man, pumping out shoddy goods, but as saviour, producing the new items which people want.

If an article goes out of style, the question of quality becomes irrelevant. The item is obsolete, even though the quality may be as new. Vance Packard quotes an American retail chairman on how fashion must accelerate, to create more rapid dissatisfaction:

> We must accelerate obsolescence…. It is our job to make women unhappy with what they have…. We must make them so unhappy that their husbands can find no happiness or peace in their excessive savings.[5]

So we have this year's 'in' colour. No fashion-conscious consumer would want to be seen in last year's. Shoe designs change, trouser pleats come and go and the tightness around the ankles moves in and out. Padded shoulders are out. Then in. We follow, because we want to be a part of the crowd. We don't like to be laughed at.

Now I don't want to knock fashion as such. I enjoy fashion; I find it an exciting part of the human potential for creativity. I find it depressing when on the continent to see Englishmen abroad. You can nearly always tell them, in their bland, unimaginative beiges and greys and shapeless trousers and shirts. By contrast, Italian and French men show more creativity, brighter colours and more sense of fun in their clothes. I like fashion a lot.

But what I object to is the creation of rapid fads of style and colour, the idea that you have to follow the crowd in buying the same, mass-produced fashion which the chain stores have in stock that season. And then you buy the new fad as that comes in and dump most of last year's.

Each year brings its novelty: Cabbage-Patch dolls, a green goo called Slime, furry cartoon characters to stick on your car windows. In 1950s America it was Davy Crockett hats. When I was at junior school it was two plastic balls on strings, which we called 'clackers', and knocked together for hours on end, until we got bored with them. If the built-in death-date doesn't get them, your boredom will as you look for the next new thing. As you buy the new things the old ones are thrown away. One of the most condemnatory expressions of our culture is 'old fashioned'. A rapid turnover in desire means a rapidly filling bin.

It will be argued that if fads were not created, people would buy less, and that jobs would be lost. But this is really a nonargument. It is as much as saying we should not have done away with hanging because it put hangmen out of work, or we should have retained thumbscrews because they kept a good manufacturing workforce in employment. Decisions about ethics and the kind of society we want must come first, and jobs will be created accordingly.

If we want a society where we mass-produce junk to throw away soon after, jobs are created to produce junk. If we want quality goods, the market responds by training more people to produce their own goods, on a smaller scale. If you are happy to buy badly-made plastic toys, that creates jobs in the trashy toy market. If you buy handmade goods, that helps support a craftsman. Prices will almost certainly be higher, but maybe our quality of life would improve if we had a few, well-produced items rather than tons of junk.

We currently consume about 40 times as much as a Somali villager. But does this make us 40 times as happy? Or even the smallest bit happier? I doubt it.

The idea that newest is best is a symptom of a wider attitude in our culture, which C.S. Lewis referred to as 'chronological snobbism'. This is the view which says that in all areas of life, that which follows must be an improvement on that which went before. It is a kind of popularised evolutionary theory which assumes that things are always improving. Hence, Jakob Bronowski wrote a book entitled *The Ascent of Man*, the very title implying mankind's progress is necessarily onward and upward to greater things. Whilst many today would object to the sexism of the title, few would query the assumption that mankind's journey has been an ascent. It is an idea fixed in the popular mind.

Professor Stephen Hawking, author of the best-selling *A Brief History of Time*, shares the assumption. When he wrote an account for *The Independent* (31st December 1988) on the background to his own thinking, he cited Bronowski as one of his heroes, saying that *The Ascent of Man* had given him 'a feeling for the achievement of the human race in developing from primitive savages only 15,000 years ago, to our present state. Hawking ends his book by expressing the hope that enlightened mankind is not far off knowing the mind of God.

In reality, the supposed development of humans from near-animal to near-God is one of the myths of the modern West. As G.K. Chesterton pointed out, in his off-beat history of mankind, *The Everlasting Man*, we know very little about the cave-man. What we do know for sure is not that he was bestial, ignorant, immoral, or that he dragged his wife around by the hair, but that he chose to paint cows on the walls of his living room; an action which hardly marks him out as a 'savage'.

A culture which has produced Belsen, Chernobyl, Hiroshima, ecological disaster on a global scale, vast world poverty and more wars this century than any other century in recorded history looks slightly ridiculous telling the cave-man who sits with his paint pot that he is a savage.

I am drawing the parallel between popular evolutionism and consumerism to show how the salesman can easily call upon popular 'science' to back up his claims. C.S. Lewis wrote, in an essay on the 'Great Myth' of evolutionism and its links with consumerism,

> Nothing *ought* to last. They want you to have a new car, a new radio set, a new everything every year. The new model must always be superseding the old. Madam would like the *latest* fashion. For this is evolution, this is development, this is the way the universe itself is going.[6]

The salesman, then, is able to tap deep into one of the powerful myths shared by most people in the West, a myth so familiar and unquestioned that we take its truth for granted. He knows that, deep down, we are already on his side.

Pollution and Lifestyle

We need to look at our lifestyles, and at just how much you

and I are actually contributing to the problem of world pollution. One aspect of this is thinking about what goes into our rubbish bin. Dozens of items which we throw away could go to an Oxfam shop or jumble sale, and actually do some good by being resold. My own leather brief-case was fished out of a dustbin, and fifteen years later is still used every day. It was high quality, but the previous owner got bored with the style. So much we throw away could be used by somebody else. Even cardboard boxes and loo rolls will be welcomed by a local primary school, eager to have raw materials for poster-painted houses, ships and binoculars.

We throw away a great deal of food. Each year the average household throws away 290 lb of it. Sixty-five per cent of the food served in American restaurants ends up in the bin. Some of the edible rubbish we throw away is actually the most valuable part of the food. A family's annual throw-out of potato peelings contains the protein in 60 steaks, the iron in 500 eggs and the vitamin C in 95 glasses of orange juice.

Other aspects of our Western lifestyle are more directly dangerous. But so often it is only when the dangers reach our own back door that we notice the consequences of the way we live. A recent example is that of chlorofluorocarbons (CFCs), whose use in the West has gradually been destroying the ozone layer which shields the earth from cancer-causing solar radiation. Despite many years of campaigning by environmental groups such as Friends of the Earth, the ozone question only started to be taken seriously when British scientists discovered a dangerous hole in the ozone layer above the Antarctic.

The publicity given to the now-notorious CFCs alerted the public to the consequences of certain everyday products they had previously taken for granted. Many people rethought buying habits with regard to hairsprays, deodorants and other products containing CFCs. And, in response to consumer pressure, manufacturers began marketing 'ozone-friendly' products. By July 1989 Tesco had phased out all items containing CFCs and other stores were set to follow suit. The EEC had announced a complete ban on CFCs by the year 2000, and even the previously cynical Margaret Thatcher had hosted an international conference on ozone in London.

CFCs have been a relatively happy example of environmental concerns touching consumer habits in the West. But what happens when the environment and immediate self-interest are in direct conflict? This has been seen in the case of global warming, or the 'greenhouse effect', caused by carbon dioxide emissions forming a heat trap in the atmosphere. Ultimately, scientists warn, the result of such warming will be the melting of polar ice caps, flooding many regions of the world. Despite the threat of Cambridge and countless other inland UK cities becoming coastal resorts as present coastal areas flood, and despite a call from a United Nations meeting of scientists in Toronto in the summer of 1988 for all industrialised countries to reduce carbon dioxide emissions by fifty per cent by the year 2020, action has been slow and reluctant.

This is because most of the carbon dioxide is produced by burning fossil fuels into the atmosphere. And Britain's fossil fuel consumption is rising. The Government's own Energy Technology Support Unit says that over the next thirty years, Britain's demand for energy could rise by thirty per cent. In other words, cutting back on power generation would mean harming the economy and consumers' freedom to burn up as much fuel as they like. Consequently, the Government has been slow to act, out of a commitment to minimal government intervention (which would be necessary on a massive scale), and an obsession with economic growth. And most consumers are not willing to adopt a lifestyle which is less demanding on energy. Care for the environment – and even the wellbeing of future generations – are being jeopardised by today's consumerist mentality.

Similarly, lead in petrol is known to be responsible for fifty per cent of the lead in our atmosphere, which in turn can affect children's brain development and is a significant cause of acid rain – more of which later. But each of us can actually do something about this form of pollution, particularly now lead-free petrol is more freely available, and at a price lower than the ordinary stuff. Many cars can use lead-free, and others can be adapted quite simply to use it.

In an age where we root value and identity in purchases, careful buying of products which do not harm the environment, cause injustice to humans or cruelty to animals, or whose production does not cause pollution, is an important statement to those around us. Books such as *The Green Consumer Guide* (Gollancz, 1988) offer a helpful analysis of most everyday products from an ethical standpoint. This book makes useful recommendations so that each of us, starting in small ways, can gradually re-educate our shopping habits so we can help to buy a better world. The choices each of us makes as we stand in the supermarket have a direct effect on the natural world and people on the other side of that world. We desperately need to add justice and care to our shopping list.

Trees

Perhaps the area where the effects of consumerism on the environment can be seen most clearly is with trees, both our trees at home and those in distant countries. Our lifestyles profoundly affect both. An area of tropical rainforest the size of Great Britain is felled every year to provide the world with paper. This doesn't include all the other areas also used for paper, such as Canada and Asia.

The Amazon region contains one third of all the world's trees. But more than 40 per cent of the Amazon's rain forests have been destroyed in the last century. If the present rate continues, there will not be a great deal left by the end of the century, disappearing as it is at 100 acres per minute.

In a year, each family in Britain puts around six trees' worth of paper into the bin. In his book *Trees*, the environmentalist Andreas Feiniger points out that one extra-large edition of the New York Times left a 360-acre gap in the forest – the wood of 77,000 trees.

It is not just paper which uses up forest. Amazonia contains some 100,000 cattle ranches, to keep the West supplied with beef for burgers and steaks. MacDonalds states it only uses American beef. Nonetheless, other fast food companies are responsible for a massive amount of ecological mayhem. And it still takes 800 square miles of forest to keep MacDonalds in paper for one year!

Another user of forest is tobacco. It has been claimed that 300 cigarettes consume one Third World tree. This is for 'curing' the tobacco – exposing it to a constant temperature of 160 degrees for about a week. Peter Taylor, in *The Smoke Ring* draws the following conclusions:

> A quick calculation shows why the horizons are bare: the average size of a tobacco allotment in Rio Grande Do Sul (Brazil) is about four acres. Therefore, in one year, the area's 100,000 tobacco farmers need the wood of 60 million trees – or nearly 1.5 million acres of forest.[7]

And this is only in that area of Brazil.

Our rapid consumption of the world's forests is particularly ironic, in view of the fact that much of it is not actually necessary. At present, only 25 per cent of the world's paper is recycled. It has been estimated that if we doubled that amount and recycled half the paper currently used, we would meet almost 75 per cent of the world's demand for new paper. A report by Washington-based group Worldwatch says that recycling can cut the energy used in paper production by between 50 and 90 per cent, when compared with using trees.

The usual complaint is that recycling is uneconomic. But when the growing global ecological crisis is added into the equation, what is truly uneconomic? The point is coming where governments will have to take recycling more seriously, otherwise the rainforests simply won't be there to plunder.

Recycling has generally been seen as the province of green bumpkins with a (wood) chip on their shoulder. But it is a field where all of us should be taking a greater involvement. It is particularly an area where groups, such as youth groups, schools and churches can pool resources to help and even make some money in doing so. Christian Aid have produced a helpful booklet, *Recycling for Change, a Handbook for Fundraising by Recycling*. The main way you and I can help, this very week, is by re-educating our buying habits to include recycled writing paper, envelopes and even loo rolls (note: recycled loo rolls mean those using recycled paper!). As consumer demand for recycled goods rises, it will become more economic to recycle.

It is not only the rainforests that are being harmed. Trees are also affected much closer to home. According to Friends of the Earth, two thirds of Britain's oaks and over half of its beeches are severely damaged by air pollution. This results in leaf-loss, bark splitting, dieback and abnormal growth. Even the Forestry Commission's own report says that only 44 per cent of Britain's trees can be classified as healthy, and that is in a country near the bottom of the league of the quantity of land under trees. And since 1947 no less than 190,000 miles of hedgerows have vanished from England and Wales, mostly uprooted in the name of large-scale agribusiness.

The causes of the pollution are the sulphur emissions from coal-fired power stations and car exhausts. Action is needed. All EEC countries pledged themselves to cut sulphur emissions by 60 per cent by 1995 – except the UK. And each of us contributes in a tiny way to the problem when we drive out using unleaded petrol or leave on the electricity for longer than is necessary.

Trees are not only a matter of beauty. They are also about human survival. Trees produce the oxygen humans need to survive. The Amazon is estimated to produce nearly half of the earth's total oxygen, and has been described as 'the lungs of the planet'. The consumer society could be cutting off its own life-support machine.

Forests also sustain life inside themselves. It is estimated that as more and more rainforest is cleared, at least one species is made extinct every four hours, many of which could have medical advantages useful to people. Around one fifth of the planet's animal and plant species could disappear in the next twenty years.

As forest land is cleared of trees, the soil is no longer bound together by the trees' roots. Soil erosion is caused within five years, as rain sweeps in. Deforestation is a major cause of floods. Until recent years 70 per cent of Sudan was under forest. Today much of the country is desert, and this is thought to be a significant factor in the tragic 1988 floods in that country. Many so-called 'natural disasters' have in fact a very human origin. Every year, another 15 million acres of land on the earth becomes desert, leaving it more vulnerable to the effects of harsh weather conditions. Much of this is because of deforestation and the effects of overfarming land, leaving it dead and unproductive.

The other loss to life on the planet as we clear more trees is less tangible. It is a loss of the sense of mystery, the unexplored and unknown. The creed of the consumer society is that mankind is sovereign, that he is pushing back the frontiers of knowledge, creating ever more wonderful goods and ever greater freedom of choice for himself. In the pursuit of this goal he has a right to rape the natural world, and to brush aside ancient notions of awe before nature. It is a kind of technological pornography, in which the subject, nature, is demystified and becomes another consumer good, unable to retain modesty and secrecy. Domination of nature is an extension of the modern dream that mankind is king, and his throne is made from the ravaged materials of the natural world.

Christianity and Nature

Christianity has sometimes been taken as a justification of the pillage of nature. Unlike earlier pagan religions, the Christians did not see nature itself as divine. Many pre-Christian religions and Eastern religions had a pantheistic view of the world which saw gods in the rivers, trees and seas. To desecrate nature was to tread on divine toes. The pantheists said, and still say in Eastern religions, that because god is everything and everything is god, the point of life is to rid oneself of the illusion that the individual is separate from the nature around it. Nature is not only god, it is a part of your very self.

Much of the mysticism in the inner circle of the modern ecology movement is based on this same pantheism. There is talk of 'earth-mother' figures, personification of nature as the goddess Gaia or Diana, and some have a longing for a supposedly idyllic druidic culture, where nature embodied the divine spark and is revered. The ecologists are reacting against the materialistic view of existence which would reduce everything to mere chemical formulae and cost-efficiency. The pantheists assert that it is only seeing nature as divine that we can restore its mystery and majesty.

Against this pantheism, ancient and modern, Christianity stated firmly that God created nature, but is separate from his creation. When you look at a flower you are looking at divine handiwork, but not a piece of God. There is some truth in the claim that Christianity's desacralisation (stripping away of the sacred) of nature meant people had fewer qualms about exploiting it. After all, Genesis says that humankind was given dominion over nature. According to this view, pantheism had given nature a dignity which Christianity stripped away, leaving it simply as a great mine to be dug.

This view has also been bolstered by a popularly held dualistic view of Christianity which identifies all aspects of the created world as evil, because they are 'material' and not 'spiritual'. Anything physical is of less value than the spiritual. Earthly existence, according to this view, is there to be risen above by contemplation of heaven. One day Christ will return, the earth will be destroyed and God's people will be whisked off to heaven.

But this interpretation fails to do justice to the biblical material on the environment. God saw his creation and declared it to be 'very good'. Dominion, which has been interpreted as 'domination', in fact means a kind of responsible stewardship, which tends and cares. Adam and Eve were gardeners, not Vikings set loose to pillage. A tree is not an inanimate object, but a fellow-creature bearing the imprint of the same creator. St Paul, in his letter to Rome, reminds us that nature gives people an insight into the very character of God.[8] Mankind is not owner, but steward, who will one day be called to account for the quality of his stewardship.

The dualistic interpretation of Christianity is based on Greek philopsophy rather than on the Bible. The Greeks rigidly separated the spiritual from the material, elevated one and despised the other, and this dualism was fed into Christian theology. This is a distortion of the God of the Bible, who creates and affirms his creation. All of life – spiritual, sexual, emotional, financial, eating, going shopping – can be lived in response to God. He created a rabbit or a blade of grass not just to make a 'spiritual' point, but because it has value in itself.

Similarly, after the fall, it is not just a disembodied 'spirit' or 'soul' which can be saved, but the whole person. This includes the physical aspects as much as the more obviously spiritual ones. God is interested in how we spend our money, whether we care about injustice, the environment, and so on. All of life is being redeemed. In this sense, Christianity is extremely 'worldly', because it attaches great importance to physical existence and the lifestyles we adopt, in a way which 'other-worldly' expressions of religion do not.

We need a rediscovery of the holistic Christianity which affirms every dimension of life and which is sensitive to the world around it, seeing (to quote the Canadian singer Bruce Cockburn) 'rumours of glory' all around us. We need to rediscover a God who not only delights in prayer and contemplation, but in food, music, sex and trees – because he invented them all in the first place.

In this we may have much to learn from the world-views of cultures different from our own. Jonathon Porritt, director of Friends of the Earth, quotes from a letter sent in 1855 to the US Government by the chief of the Dwamish Indians, in response to an offer to buy some of their land:

> How can you buy or sell the sky? We do not own the freshness of the air or the sparkle on the water. How then can you buy them from us? Every part of the Earth is sacred to my people, holy in their memory and experience. We know that the white man does not understand our ways. He is a stranger who comes in the night, and takes from our land whatever he needs. The Earth is not his friend but his enemy, and when he's conquered it, he moves on. He kidnaps the Earth from his children. His appetite will devour the Earth and leave behind a desert.[9]

Pollution and World-View

At the end of the day, our attitude towards the environment is determined by our world-view. The major world-view of consumerism is one of growth, expansion and the production of ever more sophisticated means of satisfying human sensual desires. To keep the economy growing, more goods must be produced and hence consumed. Short life and disposability are positive virtues. Ever-increasing consumption must be stimulated through advertising. To quote Jonathon Porritt, 'the only way to beat a glut is to turn everybody into gluttons'.[10]

However, this world-view has two serious flaws. One is that the earth's resources are finite. You can only extract so much coal from a mine, oil from the sea, paper from the forests. And you can only pump so much waste into a dustbin. Our consumer lifestyles, which behave as if there is no tomorrow, will come up against an immovable wall: the earth has limits. Enough is enough. If everyone in the world consumed at the rate of the Americans, this would use up to twelve times the current amount of natural resources being consumed globally. The earth's oil supplies would run out in just seven years. And if the world consumed at the rate of the British, the oil would last around fourteen years. The politics of consumerism simply don't work because they assume that unlimited growth and prosperity are not only desirable but possible. We desperately need to explore – to use the ecologists' term – more sustainable development.

The second flaw is what happens to human beings in the process. When we are constantly exhorted to keep our rate of consumption up, and that not to do so is unpatriotic, antisocial or plain eccentric, what does that do to our sense of priorities? We become increasingly blasé about sensual experience and demand ever new stimulations to keep us amused. Life is a search after new products, new stimulation. We lose a sense of reverence for the world around us – it is the bin into which we drop our rubbish. We lose sight of an older wisdom which told us that moderation was a virtue, that sometimes we had to do without things, and that some pleasures were only to be enjoyed occasionally.

We demand an ever increasing standard of life, merrily ignoring the fact that as we pollute creation and drain the dregs of its riches and live individualistic, self-seeking lives, we actually lose genuine fullness of life. We become angry babies, demanding to be pampered, screaming if we are not warm, well fed and being constantly tickled.

Notes

[1] *World Conservation Strategy* (International Union for the Conservation of Nature Resources: Switzerland, 1980).

[2] John Elkington and Julia Hailes, *The Green Consumer Guide* (Gollancz: London, 1988) p 8.

[3] Jon Vogler, 'The Bottle Bank Con Trick', *New Internationalist* (March 1986) p 26.

[4] *Ibid*.

[5] Vance Packard, *The Waste Makers* (Penguin: London, 1960) p 74.

[6] C.S. Lewis, 'The Funeral of a Great Myth', *Christian Reflections* (Fount: London, 1981) p 122.

[7] Peter Taylor, *The Smoke Ring* (Sphere: London, 1984) p 252.

[8] Romans 1:20.

[9] Quoted in Jonathon Porritt, *Seeing Green* (Basil Blackwell: Oxford, 1984) p 184.

[10] *Ibid*.

8

POP, POLITICS AND PACKAGING

Selling People as Products

The Hollywood Dream

The face and body of Marilyn Monroe proved to be notorious. Not the face and body of a mere human being, who read the paper, sweated and walked the dog, but those of Marilyn – symbol, goddess, legend.

In medieval art the icons of the Virgin Mary inspired contemplation and devotion. Someday historians will look back at our century and will see our icons to Marilyn. Like the Virgin, Marilyn's portraits – on the walls of chic restaurants, in coffee table books, on mirrors, posters and post cards – point to something beyond herself, to the American Dream, to the culture which had the genius to get men on to the moon and invent Coke, rock'n'roll and Hollywood.

It was the glitter of Hollywood which had attracted a young girl called Norma Jeane Baker. Insecure, vulnerable and brought up in a series of foster homes, Norma Jeane would escape into the glittering, pimple-free Hollywood fantasy. Like the heroine in Woody Allen's *Purple Rose of Cairo*, she longed for the image she saw onscreen of fame, desire and beautiful people. In real life, friends called her 'the mouse'. In her fantasies she was different, a part of the Hollywood dream. Playing on uncertainty about the identity of her father, she would even call Clark Gable her 'secret father'.

Determined to make the fantasy a reality, Norma Jeane Baker moved into modelling and walk-on parts in films. She dyed her hair blonde. She exercised for at least forty minutes every day, had dental treatment to correct her rabbity front teeth and wore a brace for several hours a day, paying for the treatment on credit. The final touch was to have cosmetic surgery to remove two blemishes on her chin. Some biographers claim she also had a lump from the end of her nose removed and cartilage added to her jaw to strengthen her jaw line.

And Norma Jeane Baker changed her name to Marilyn Monroe. In the words of one of her many biographers, Joan Mellen:

> The image of exaggerated sexuality projected by Monroe was thus entirely a creation of herself and of her Hollywood advisors packaging a product and putting together a sex symbol with surgical knife, bandages, and bodily distortion.[1]

The words, 'packaging a product' are significant. For the whole of her traumatic and well-documented life, Marilyn was a divided personality. She frequently spoke of Norma Jeane and Marilyn as two different people. Behind the product, being marketed as you might market clothes or a new car – as an object of envy and desire – hid Norma Jeane, still shy and insecure, longing for respect and love as a person, not as a consumer durable. Referring to the success of *Gentlemen Prefer Blondes* in 1953, Marilyn explained that it was almost as if Norma could stand aside and watch the success of Marilyn, the product: 'I feel it's all happening to someone right next to me. I'm close, I can feel it, I can hear it, but it isn't really me.' And later, 'A sex symbol becomes a thing – I just hate to be a thing.'

Packaging the Presidency

The advertising man is not content to create a dreamscape in order to sell us the food for our supper and the glide-on sticks for our armpits. He also packages people for our consumption. Or perhaps, more accurately, he sells us an image of the person as we would like to believe they are. He sells us an idealised package. Far more desirable than a real person who loses their temper, gets spots and burps. It is this illusion which is at the heart not only of Hollywood and the entire pop industry, but of the politics of power, particularly the stateside variety.

In the 1952 American presidential elections a wily Eisenhower, then Republican candidate, decided that there was no reason why a politician should not be sold in the same way as a packet of cigarettes. He bought one and a half million dollars of TV advertising.

After the 1960 televised debate between presidential candidates Kennedy and Nixon the radio audience, who had heard and evaluated all the arguments, judged that Nixon had come out on top. At the same time the 70 million strong TV audience, seeing the image of Nixon's sweating face next to Kennedy's boyish good looks, concluded that Kennedy had won hands down. Similarly, during the 1980 debate between Carter and Reagan, Carter's rhetoric and content was judged by the audience in the hall to be superior to Reagan's. But that isn't how it appeared on TV. Reagan was two inches taller than Carter and this was the overriding image which remained in the mind. This physical difference was underlined when a chortling, winking Reagan came out with a witty put-down of Carter, the sort of image which stuck in the mind of smalltown America.

The relative importance of medium and message in politics has been changing over the last three decades. Image matters more and more – the content of what is being said, seemingly less and less. Today it would be practically unthinkable to elect an ugly politician. A survey in 1987 from the University of California claimed that a politician with flat cheekbones, angular jaw and eyes rounded at the top can count on five to ten per cent more votes.

Nixon

When Nixon re-entered politics in 1968, his words about packaging offered a telling glimpse behind the scenes of modern politics: 'I was resolved to rely on my TV producer. How you look on TV is more important than what you say. Candidates with the best TV advisers are generally the candidates who prevail.' In other words, candidates sold as a consumer package were more likely to succeed than those who relied solely on the merits of their arguments. The introduction of TV did away at a stroke with the significance of mass rallies, except when they would make good TV. A few well-planned minutes on the box, carefully pieced together in the same way as an any other commercial, could achieve more than a hundred such rallies. In Nixon's own words, 'If one learns to use it (television) effectively, it can be a very powerful instrument in going over the heads of Congress, going over the heads of the Washington media and so forth, directly to the people.' In the 1972 elections the Republican Party (Nixon) convention was perceived in a markedly better light than that of the Democrats (McGovern). The reason was that the Republican convention was organised to fit in exactly with the TV news timetables.

Once Nixon was elected he developed his media strategy. His visits to China and the USSR were timed to get maximum coverage on prime time TV. Heads of state do not travel abroad simply for the love of diplomacy or seeing the world. They also travel because they know it will receive massive media coverage back home. Abroad, they will probably be seen more on the home screens than when they are in their own capital city. Just over two months before the 1987 general election, Margaret Thatcher flew to Moscow. She met Russian crowds, argued with Soviet TV interviewers who were plainly taken aback by her vehemence, and held painstakingly stage-managed talks with dissidents. The impression conveyed to the watching world, including the British voters as they sat in their Basingstoke semi, was of a proud and powerful leader, well able to speak on behalf of the western world.

This was a leaf from Nixon's media book. Years earlier the President had deliberately delayed his return flight from China for five hours in Iceland, so that the triumphal homecoming would happen during the national news broadcasts.

When the pop group Wham! made their much publicised tour of China in 1984, it was not because they had exhausted the adoring adolescents of the West and were in search of paddyfields new. The trip, which cost $1.5 million, was almost entirely a publicity stunt to break the band in to the USA via the national news coverage of the visit. As George Michael strolled meaningfully along the Great Wall of China watched by the world's press the sounds in his ears were not the chimes of oriental gongs or the clatter of rickshaws but the jangle of US cash registers.

Reagan

Ronald Reagan's credentials to be a TV president were impeccable. He had a rugged Hollywood actor's figure and a reassuring, paternal voice. Every inch one of the fantasies which filled the youth of Marilyn Monroe. His advisers would carefully stage 'photo-opportunities', which would ensure wide media coverage, but with only a small risk of having questions of policy fired at him.

His speeches were planned to be full of ten-to-thirty-second 'sound-bites', witty quotes which broadcasters could easily edit out and use in isolation. When the President's eyes started to twinkle, his head leaned slightly to one side and he sighed, you knew a well-rehearsed, quotable quote was on the way. As an actor, Ronald Reagan had promoted a certain brand of shirts. His avuncular presence made you certain they were shirts you could trust. As a president, even more than in his days as an actor, it was Reagan who was the package. According to one of Reagan's aides, he spent two-thirds of his time as president on public relations and a third on policy matters.[2]

Reagan's 1984 election film, made for TV, saw the most powerful man in the West walking into the distance, together with his wife Nancy. BBC *Panorama*'s Michael Cockerell described the scene: 'She gave a flirtatious little skip and on cue he gently but firmly put his arm around her shoulder as the syrupy violins played. "I just can't imagine life without her," breathed the President, filmed in soft focus and scarce able to restrain a tear. It was the ultimate synthesis of the actor turned politician.'[3]

Likewise, Reagan's much-publicised visit to a quaint Irish pub in the home of his ancestors was stage-managed to an extent which the Royal Shakespeare Company would have been proud of. Nothing was left to chance. It never was. All his speeches, personal appearances, gestures, facial expressions and intonations were meticulously planned down to the tiniest detail by media advisers – or, to use another term, his ad men. When he made a public appearance, such as chatting to students or to primary school pupils, the questioners were exhaustively rehearsed and the President worked from a script. The nightmare of the political publicist is the unprepared question, the unrehearsed appearance, and so every effort was made to keep these to an absolute minimum. Lyn

Nofziger, Reagan media adviser:

> When you're running for president you do what you're good at. Ronald Reagan is very good at television. Obviously we ran the campaign on TV and we restricted his contact with the press. Of course we did. We didn't want him to screw up.[4]

Never one to miss a good publicity opportunity, Reagan contacted the Queen with regard to a visit to Britain he was about to make. He asked if she would mind if he and Mrs Windsor could be filmed strolling around the gardens of Buckingham Palace together, having a jovial tête-à-tête. The Queen refused. 'This is,' she reminded him, 'a private occasion.'[5]

Bush and Beyond

In the 1988 US Election between Bush and Dukakis the real winner was the marketing man. The ground was fertile for him to ply his trade on a scale unknown even during the Reagan years. By common consent, the campaign was between two essentially bland candidates, neither of whom stood out or excited the public. It was the perfect challenge for an industry used to giving personality to otherwise undifferentiated soft drinks, cosmetics and floor cleaners.

Both candidates surrounded themselves with media advisers. The main producers of the two campaigns were described by BBC Radio 4's American commentator Alistair Cooke as, respectively, 'a whizz of a motor car salesman' and 'a man paid to make people switch from one brand of cola to another'. The two campaigns each spent around $30 million on TV commercials.

The entire campaign was manipulated to the tiniest detail by the presidential image-makers. Every shot and quote allowed to the media was carefully planned and rehearsed, evey word scripted for effect. Candidates' faces were lit by studio lighting, even when they were out of doors, so they would look their best on TV. Any possibility of a spontaneous or unexpected statement or question was removed. The election of the world's most powerful national leader was carried out at the level of ads for rival toothpastes. The US media rapidly became disillusioned by the level of manipulation of their quarry by advisers. Some even bought loud-hailers and binoculars in an attempt to spot or stimulate the slightest unscripted reaction.

But, as far as Bush was concerned, the packaging paid off. The Bush 'handlers', as they became known, transformed their product from a minor brand seventeen percentage points behind its rival to the market leader in a matter of months. An image was advertised to the US public and they bought it. Bush the wimp, trailing in the opinion polls, was transformed in the popular mind into Bush the strong, resolute future president.

Marketing Margaret

When Reagan stood for re-election in 1984, his experts in people-packaging learned a trick or two from the other side of the Atlantic. Republican campaign managers watched with fascination a video of a 1983 BBC TV *Panorama* programme, *The Marketing of Margaret*. Margaret Thatcher was no stranger to marketing. Brought up as a grocer's daughter in Grantham, she knew the value of presentation in selling a product.

Having learned the lessons of US presidential campaigns, she used strong visual images, perfect for TV, which remained in the mind. On one occasion she took a banknote and snipped it down the middle with a pair of scissors. 'This is what the pound in your pocket is worth under Labour', she warned grimly. Photo-opportunities were carefully planned. It was Mrs Thatcher's media man, Gordon Reece, who introduced the American-style photo-opportunity to the UK in 1979, when he posed Maggie hugging a young calf (the calf, as if in mute bovine protest, subsequently died). She changed her hairstyle. She worked hard at lowering her speaking voice so that when she appeared in the broadcast media she would sound less like an angry nanny.

The names Saatchi and Saatchi have become synonymous with the success of the Conservative Party in recent years. The advertising agency were first employed by the Conservative party for the 1979 election. The Saatchis were responsible for the famous posters which showed a massive queue outside a dole office, bearing the message, 'Labour Isn't Working'. They presented the Conservative party as guardians of choice, freedom and prosperity, and worked on ways of undermining the traditional Labour vote. Margaret Thatcher was regularly filmed in markets doing her shopping. She was the housewives' choice; you could almost hear Jean and Doreen in Clapham sighing with relief that at last, here was a politician who knew the price of potatoes and understood ordinary working people.

We now take it for granted that the Conservative Party conferences are pure media spectacular, from the carefully organised and televisual stage sets to the beautifully orchestrated standing ovations. An illusion is given of complete unanimity, of a party united and knowing where it is going under the command of a strong and charismatic figure. As an observer at the 1987 Conservative conference in Blackpool, I didn't find it hard to spot the political cracks in this wall whitewashed over for the media to see. Just the night before the Prime Minister's final rousing speech to the faithful the Conservative Family Campaign declared itself to be utterly opposed to party policy on Sunday trading. Other delegates told me of their unhappiness about plans for the introduction of the Poll Tax to replace domestic rates. I even met a representative of Conservatives Against Nuclear Weapons.

Perhaps the ultimate in political showbiz razzmatazz were

the major Thatcher speeches during the 1987 election, as described by political journalist Rodney Tyler:

> From the moment the lights go down and the dry-ice fog billows out into the audience (as though it were a pop concert rather than a political rally) the audience is stunned into receptivity. The impression of pop is continued with a five-minute laser show which flashes messages like 'Three Times Maggie' and 'Five More Years' into the audience to a thundering piece of modern music... From the lasers the music switches immediately to Andrew Lloyd-Webber and the Dallas-heroic campaign theme tune and the video clips of her meeting world leaders and making speeches plays on two massive screens, leaving the audience applauding wildly before she has even started.[6]

The Left Latches on

Parties of the left have almost always been slower to realise the persuasive potential of salesmanship, perhaps due to a deep-seated socialist suspicion that slick marketing trivialises the message being conveyed and because they hold a basic faith in tub-thumping rhetoric. As Eisenhower was spending his $1.5 million on TV advertising in the 1952 presidential campaign, his Democrat opponent, Adlai Stevenson, spent just $76,000. Such was his mistrust of packaging that Stevenson, who fought two Presidential elections, only used his media adviser to help tune the TV set in his hotel room. During his second campaign in 1956, following the sound beating the Democrats had received four years earlier, Stevenson was heard to mutter that he disliked the way his party were adopting the marketing techniques of the opponents: he felt as if he was taking part in a beauty contest rather than a serious political debate.

In the early 1980s, as Tories were applying the marketing machine to British politics, Labour was still relying on the

Welsh Valleys oratory of Michael Foot, surely one of the least glamorous politicians ever to have set foot in Westminster. The one notable exception to this rule was Harold Wilson, who demonstrated a pre-Reaganite adeptness at presenting a saleable face to the media. When he decided to give the Beatles OBEs, it was not just the Liverpool moptops who came off well from the publicity stunt. The Prime Minister was cashing in on the fact that, in the words of American poet Allen Ginsberg, Liverpool was 'the present centre of the consciousness of the human universe.' All this, claimed the stunt, was thanks to the nation's groovy Prime Minister.

But by the 1987 election, Labour as a party were catching on. They had to face the harsh truth that their choice was to play the marketing game or remain forever a party of opposition. Neil Kinnock was the first British party leader to be chosen in large part for his media abilities. He felt at ease in the medium of television. One of his first tasks as newly-elected party leader was to appoint a media adviser. Not long after, Neil Kinnock was to be seen with wife Glenys at West End plays, premieres (such as that of the film Absolute Beginners) and exclusive parties where tabloid paparazzi were guaranteed to be lurking behind curtains, telephoto lenses at the ready.

Labour changed the official party colour from a slightly Leninist red to a respectable, trustworthy beige, with a red rose motif. Kinnock was spotted in a pop video with singer and comedienne Tracey Ullmann, as if to say to Thatcherite Britain, 'Look! I'm relating to the youth of today!' The crowning glory was the Labour Party election film, made by Hugh Hudson, director of the feature film Chariots of Fire. It was truly the point at which Hollywood met Westminster, a weepie to compare with Love Story and ET. To a backing of stirring music, Neil and Glenys wandered hand in hand across windswept cliffs and looked emotionally at old photo albums. And it worked. Kinnock's personal rating shot up by sixteen per cent in just seven days.

Margaret had turned British politics into show business, previously considered unthinkably American by sober minded Englishmen. Neil, armed with photo albums and walking boots, had to perform his turn or be thrown off the stage of British politics. Labour fought the 1987 election not on the socialist policies decided at their Party Conference, but on the personality of Neil and Glenys, Britain's answer to Ronnie and Nancy. Even Mrs Thatcher was taken aback by the way Labour had relied on the ad-men: 'Labour was all packaging – merely packaging politics like some washing powder. What an irony that they were using capitalist tools like advertising and so on and not getting down to the nitty gritty.'[7]

The message of the Peter Sellers film, *Being There*, is no longer so absurd: that of a head of government being elected not because of his abilities as a statesman, but because he speaks in simple, picturesque phrases and looks the part.

It must be said that in Britain the extent of potential media manipulation is not what it is in the USA. Unlike America we have an influential national press. TV does not have the same stranglehold since the UK has a strong, viable alternative source of national news. Such a press has been impractical on the other side of the Atlantic, due to the size of the country and the consequent difficulties of daily distribution. In the UK there are stricter laws governing the access of political parties to TV advertising. And Britain, unlike the USA, has a parliamentary Question Time in which the head of government is put on the spot regularly and made to justify him or herself publicly.

We relish the moments, and quite rightly, when an interviewer such as Robin Day verbally savages a prominent politician and forces him face-to-face to justify policies or statements. It is in moments like this when some degree of reality intrudes into the selling machine. We detect every attempt at evading the question, every desperate 'Well, let me just make *this* point', every unrehearsed and unscripted reaction, every touch of fallible humanity. But the general point remains: the images conveyed by TV increasingly dominate the political process in the West.

The Soviet bloc joined in the performance. Even the meticulously packaged Reagan was upstaged during the December 1987 arms summit by a media-conscious Gorbachev. The Soviet leader won the hearts of the West by his media appearances. You almost forgot he was the head of a totalitarian state.

The Power of the Package

Just as politicians in previous eras learned the rules of rhetoric in order to persuade by words, so modern-day politicians have developed a range of techniques suited to television, in order to persuade by image. One method of ensuring greater coverage has been used to great effect by Labour's Denis Healey in TV discussions. It involves laughing excessively and waving your hands when your opponent makes a point. Because TV debate thrives on conflict and reaction, the director then turns the camera on you, to use these moments of reaction as 'cutaways', and the audience at home misses the full force of the opponent's point. All they can see is you ridiculing it.

Another trick was used by Lord Young in a pre-election edition of the BBC's *This Week Next Week*. After a seemingly lacklustre performance for most of the programme, the final five minutes saw him liven up and deliver a selection of major points, even interrupting the interviewer to put them across with force. His reason, when questioned on this by colleagues afterwards, was that the programme was followed by *Eastenders*. Five million soap opera viewers, who would be voting in a few weeks' time, would have switched on their sets for the final five minutes of the previous programme.

One of the most thought-provoking pieces of TV drama in recent years was a BBC play called *The Vision*, directed by Norman Stone. A middle-aged TV presenter, played by Dirk

Bogarde, is offered a £2,000 a week job in a new, slightly sinister satellite religious broadcasting network, the People Channel. He is offered the post because he has the sort of warm, reassuring voice which would best convey the suave, comforting blend of religion and family values the channel purports to convey. Helen, his wife, is a Christian. When she asks the Controller how her husband, a non-believer, can speak and persuade others of religious truth, she is told: 'Television is images, Mrs Marriner. What matters is the effect we have. Actions not intentions. If James Marriner on television convinces one viewer of the truth, what does it matter that he has doubts of his own?' Form triumphs over content.

When Marriner is found to be having an extramarital affair, the channel is prepared to keep it quiet because he is a good media figurehead. Image is everything. Public perception counts for more than personal integrity. At the end, Marriner's reputation is ruined when his adultery is made public, his mistress kills herself and the People Channel is revealed to be a propagandistic right-wing political group which will go from strength to strength. But at the heart of the brokenness of James Marriner's life is a message of hope. The suffering has started a process of healing. Marriner the TV personality had become a victim of the medium. He had been a glamorously packaged star, a facade with little behind it. The reality behind the illusion had been a life which had lost true humanity and intimacy with those closest to him. Life consisted of opening supermarkets, dreaming of past glories and the surreptitious thrills of adultery. Even spirituality was a saleable commodity thanks to the People Channel. Tragedy ripped away the illusion and revealed the man beneath, a man insecure and empty, a man obscured by packaging.

In Manchester Art Gallery there is a massive canvas of Marilyn Monroe's face, printed many times in gaudy primary colours. It is almost as if a machine has produced it. In fact it was the 'pop' artist Andy Warhol in the 60s. It is reminiscent of his pictures of soup cans, painted in the same style. Both Marilyn and the soup cans are celebrated as aspects of the same junk culture: both attractively packaged, production line units: to be bought and enjoyed, but ultimately disposable. Norma Jeane Baker could stand aside and look at Marilyn, the character created by her own fantasies and the Hollywood marketing men.

When Marilyn put together a photo album for a friend's birthday, she included a shot of herself looking out of a window. A shot looking as if she had just got up, her face half-serious, her lips together, unlike the temptress Marilyn of the screen. She wrote next to the photograph, 'This is my favorite.'

Prepackaged Pop: The Monkees

Alongside Marilyn and the presidency, the US marketing triumph of the 60s was the Monkees. Beatlemania had the West in its sweaty, adolescent grip and the four Liverpudlians were proving to be one of the UK's most profitable exports. America, inventor of rock'n'roll, realised they were missing out on something big.

So they began with a marketing concept: four good looking lads who could act, a TV series and a clutch of songs so catchy the world would be humming them the moment they heard them. Auditions were held for the Monkees, the prepackaged teen idols who would appear in 10 million homes. Four hundred people were interviewed and candidates were selected less for musical ability than for cheeky smiles and charisma. Those rejected included people who were later to become well known as more serious musicians, such as Steven Stills (later of Crosby, Stills, Nash and Young). Songs were written by top songwriters of the day, rarely by the band members themselves. Neil Diamond provided *I'm a Believer* and *A Little Bit Me, A Little Bit You*. Goffin and King wrote the wonderful *Pleasant Valley Sunday*. And, most controversially, the group did not even play the instruments on their own records.

The 1966 press release from NBC TV guaranteed 'the funniest revolt against our conforming button-down society that has yet come to television.' The Monkees' theme tune boasted, 'We're the young generation and we've got something to say.' In truth, the band were the conception of the very consumer society which 60s youth were supposed to be rebelling against. And unlike Dylan, the Beatles, the Byrds and other bands of mid-1966, they weren't achieving very much at all in the way of self-expression.

By 1967 the product started rebelling against its producers. The carefully assembled package started to realise it was little more than a money spinner and that their one claim to greatness was the brilliant songs, which were no more their own than the musicianship on the records. For the members of the Monkees who wanted to be taken seriously as musicians (particularly guitarist Michael Nesmith who had previously been a folk singer, calling himself Michael Blessing), enough was enough. The band slipped into the emerging psychedelic music scene, the counter-culture and the Summer of Love, seeing in protest songs and references to drugs the authenticity they had been denied in their days as a supermarket product.

It is significant that, five years after the death of Marilyn, due at least in part to her inability to resolve the tensions between a packaged public persona and an insecure self longing for authenticity, America's next mass-market human package rebelled similarly. The Image of God in humanity was being squeezed into the mould of a golden calf and the image was feeling the pain.

Fleece the World

Twenty years after the Monkees there was an almost identical attempt at pop packaging for big bucks. This time it was in London. As with the Monkees, this package was to be pure pop hype, pure image, an arousal of hysteria by a bunch of people who had never played a note together. In the late 1970s, Tony James had played alongside a young Billy Idol in the punk rock group Generation X. As the 70s became the 80s Idol cultivated a sneer and went West to seek fame and fortune. The Americans loved him and he stayed.

James stayed in Britain working on the Master Plan, the formation of a group whose visual impact would be so great and their press manipulation so successful that they would be heralded as the future of rock'n'roll. All this before they entered a recording studio. Tony James borrowed the name Sigue Sigue Sputnik from a Moscow street gang, chose group members for the size of their cheek-bones rather than because they could play, and dressed them up like computer-age leather Zulus. He made a video of cut-up scenes of violence from his favourite futuristic video nasties and sent them to record companies. The band turned up at music industry parties in their absurd, false hairstyles and did interviews to the music press in which they spoke sinisterly of 'designer violence' and their love of films with exploding helicopters. 'We're not interested in music – we're into glamour and excitement,' Tony James explained.

They were signed by EMI records for a largeish sum, but nowhere near the million pounds figure put out to the press. Again, pure hype. But it had results. Even *The Sunday Times* carried a feature in their magazine on this new pop phenomenon which Britain's top record company considered to be worth so much. James saw Sputnik as a whole industry:

> You name it, we're going to do it. We're talking books, films, TV shows, video arcade games. We're going to be bigger than Rank. We're going to be bigger than General Motors.

The ad man had taught himself to play bass guitar, but in the 1980s he saw his skills as publicist as the more valuable of the two. Tony James's slogan, distorted from Live Aid, was 'Fleece the World'.

To underline the point that here was the band who understood and used the consumer culture, Sigue Sigue Sputnik sold the gaps between the tracks of music on their first album, *Flaunt It*, as advertising space. Just one thing appeared to have been left out of this, the ultimate consumer package – the music itself. When the first single appeared it was a disappointment of Sputnik proportions. It took a synthesised rehash of an old Eddie Cochran guitar riff and played it to death to the accompaniment of echoes and explosions. It reached number three in the pop charts, but this was almost entirely on the basis of the earlier hype and packaging.

When people looked inside the package, it became evident that they had been sold a package with virtually nothing inside. At least the Monkees had good tunes. SSS represented the ad man's dream: a 'music' group which could be sold not in concert venues and on the radio, but in glossy images which created a self-contained world. It is a glamorous, unreal world of sexuality, excitement and breathtaking style. It is a world not unlike the Hollywood dream which, like Norma Jeane Baker, most of us long to enter. But when we try to live life as a dream, as Marilyn found, we are constantly interrupted by the cold light of day breaking in through the window. Sigue Sigue Sputnik appeared on TV's *The Tube* at the peak of their pre-musical hype. After James had expounded his sales talk on why his band were the future of rock'n'roll, the interviewer, Muriel Gray, looked him in the eye and said in a deadpan Scottish voice, 'You look a wee bit like gonks to me.' The illusion was broken. The outside world had intruded on an ad man's private fantasy.

Packaging Pap

Sputnik faded, like countless pop packages before them, and

countless more after, and were soon in the great pedal bin of ex-pop 'phenomena'. But the Monkees and Sputnik were not isolated incidents in the world of pop. The packaging of the essentially bland and contentless is the bread and butter of the industry.

The origins of pop were in the rise of the 1950s consumer culture. For the first time teenagers had money in their jeans' pockets and were in search of an identity to buy into, off-the-peg rebellious chic. Rock'n'roll supplied not only the sound-track for teenage life in the late 50s but also its styles and images. Pop continued, in the 60s, 70s and 80s, to be fre-quently a matter of marketing image, all froth and no drink, all icing and no cake, all package with no content, from the Bay City Rollers and Little Jimmy Osmond to Bros and the endless production line of identical disco outfits packaged to fit the latest fad.

However, pop need not be that way, and at best it isn't. The forerunners of pop – gospel, blues, jazz – had their origins in the sufferings of an oppressed black people and embodied the vast range of emotions felt by that people. The music was a shout of joy, a cry of pain, a vehicle for worship and for doubts. Ironically the escapism of persecuted blacks became a largely consumer escapism for non-persecuted white teena-gers. But some pop and rock retained much of the integrity of the earlier styles, and other pop has recently started to explore its own, pre-consumer heritage. Much of the best pop is reaching back beyond the consumer 50s into an earthier experience of life's emotions. It is taking from gospel a spon-taneous, unsynthetic joy, a sense of vision and a definition of love which goes beyond sweaty kisses in the back of cars; it is taking from the blues an honesty about life's tragedies and a cry for help. It is reaching back into folk and ethnic styles from around the world to enlarge its own musical and emotional vocabulary.

The consumerising of pop is an elevation of one aspect – image – into an absolute, and the result is often shallow and oddly distant from real human experience. Now this shallowness must not just be identified with 'chart pop' music. Much jangly pop actually has depth and expresses a range of human emotions (The Beatles, Amy Grant, REM, the Smiths) and much would-be 'serious' rock is actually often just pretentious, using 'profound' but virtually meaningless verbiage to create an image of profundity (Led Zeppelin).

If the consumerising of pop is a focus on pure image, the reclaiming of pop is a rediscovery of roots. This involves a rediscovery of the musical roots of pop – which grow much deeper than the shallow loam of 50s consumer America (fun though early rock'n'roll unquestionably is). It also involves a rediscovery of the roots of human emotions and identity, which grow much deeper that a one-dimensional obsession with image and sex.

The best pop affirms that image is a fun, creative part of being human. But it denies that it is the only or even the main part. It says human life and culture have roots which we sever to our own loss. The exploration of these roots can be heard in U2, Bob Dylan, Bruce Cockburn, Al Green, Waterboys, Talking Heads, Van Morrison and Paul Simon, among others.

Our Need for the Images

Yet we would not stand for the triviality of one-dimensional pop and politics, reduced to pure, contentless image, unless it met a need in ourselves. In the absence of other strong sources of identity, many of us gladly buy off-the-peg identities of a marketed pop style. Image fills a vacuum in ourselves.

And we secretly admire the political packages we are presented. The reason Ronald Reagan spent two-thirds of his time on presentation was to live up to the public's opinion of how a president should look, speak and act. After a series of presidents who had failed to live up to the mass expectation of strength and infallibility – Ford, Carter and the discredited

Nixon – the scandals and failures of Vietnam and Watergate, and the rise of fanatical anti-Americanism in Islamic fundamentalism, the public was desperate for a president who looked like a president. We don't like failure, so we accept the deception. It makes us feel good. We get the media personalities we deserve.

But when we turn people into idols both we and the person idolised suffer, whether it is the pop star, politician, film star, writer or evangelist. We suffer because we constantly compare ourselves with an idealised image which we can never attain. We are painfully aware that we are not the idol and the more we try to be that person the clearer it becomes that we cannot succeed. And the idol suffers, because they fail to match up to expectations. They have an image, a role to act out, which can detract from their humanity. Facial blemishes are airbrushed out of photos, political rallies stage-managed to convey an illusion of certainty and perfection, teen pop idols suck their cheeks in for photos to make them look more glamorous. And a sense of their own identity can be lost in the image. They become one-dimensional: the film star embodies beauty (and gets depressed and loses self-confidence when their looks fade), the evangelist is all truth and goodness (and can't live up to the image because he is a fallen human being). The idolatry of the famous imposes unreal pressures on us and a burden on the idol which they cannot cope with.

The myth of packaging is of a perfect human, without the trivial irritations of everyday life, without the banalities of being human. We follow the lives of the gloriously packaged with an odd fascination, wondering what it must be like to be superhuman: the Queen, the President, the screen heroine, the pop idol, even the famous evangelist. Media reports of the marriages, fortunes and scandals of the famous have become the surrogate in a modern individualistic society of the community gossip of an earlier age. We take the *image* of somebody else's life and try to conform ourselves to that image. And all the time real life is ticking by. When we arrive in heaven I suspect God won't ask us why we failed to be Marilyn Monroe, James Dean, Elvis, Bono of U2, or Billy Graham, but why we failed to be fully ourselves.

More of our image bubbles need to be burst. Otherwise, we fall for the original lie whispered by a serpent in an ancient garden – that men and women can be like gods, rather than creatures whose identity can only be understood in relation to the creator whose image we bear. We long for the immortality of fame and tabloid notoriety, we long to be objects of worship, rather than people born to form relationships of care and self-giving amid the pain and triviality of everyday life. The most comprehensive biography of Marilyn Monroe is entitled *Goddess*. Packaging can be a means we use to hide our essential humanness.

Few of us are in the business of marketing ourselves professionally to a mass public. But all of us live in fear of rejection by other people, as if the moment they see what we are 'really' like, they will turn away. We need to know we are accepted and liked. We are told at school that we need to 'sell ourselves' otherwise we will never get on in life. We adopt a series of different masks to make us acceptable in each of the environments in which we move: the office, the home, the church, the party. We have become experts at the art of packaging ourselves for particular markets, never fully able to believe that we are valuable and loved without any of our masks, images or packaging.

Tony James told *Smash Hits* magazine: 'If Christ were here today he would be taking major advertising space.' In other words, he would be in the queue outside the publicist's office eager to indulge in a Hollywood-Sputnik 80s Messiah sales campaign. When Mother Teresa of Calcutta commented in a New York breakfast TV studio, 'I see that Christ is needed in television studios,' I suspect she meant something very different.

Notes

1 Joan Mellen, *Marilyn Monroe* (Star: London 1975) p 26.
2 Quoted in Michael Cockerell, 'Reagan's Greatest Gift', *The Listener* (8 November 1984) p 4.
3 *Ibid.*
4 *Ibid.*
5 Quoted in Julie Burchill, *Love It or Shove It* (Century: London 1985) p 80.
6 Rodney Tyler *Campaign!* (Grafton: London 1987) p 80.
7 Rodney Tyler *op cit* p 247.

9

THE MISSION

Consumerism and the Third World

Cola Wars

The Pepsi salesmen in the Brazilian capital, Sao Paulo, call it the Mission. It is the current drive to convert the entire population of Brazil into members of the Pepsi Generation, a mission both to unbelievers (infidels who never drink cola), heretics (the misguided who currently believe that Coke is It) and agnostics (who indulge in the occasional soft drink but without any degree of passion or commitment to a brand name).

Brazil is third in the league of world soft drinks consumption – behind the USA and Mexico. But while a Mexican drinks on average 250 8 oz bottles of fizz each year – about five bottles per person per week – and Americans guzzle a stomach-turning 690 bottles – two bottles every day for every form of human life in the States, Brazilians can only manage a paltry 150 bottles each. This works out at a mere three bottles a week. Pepsico believes that Brazilians have the character, fortitude – and gluttony – to beat the Mexicans into third place.

Perhaps the bigger obstacle to persuading Brazilians to join the Pepsi Generation is the fact that 55 per cent of Brazilian soft drinks connoisseurs already choose Coke in preference to Pepsi. To inspire retailers with the Pepsi vision Pepsico staged a mammoth sales event in a Sao Paulo shopping mall, attended by 750 trades people and featuring videos of laser guns blasting Coke cans.

It was just the lastest skirmish in the Cola Wars being fought in the media and stores of not only the developed world, but also in the poorer, developing countries of the globe. The combined cola advertising budget for the current three-year period is around £110 million in Brazil alone. Pepsi have bought the fame of Tina Turner, Michael Jackson and David Bowie to promote their product in South America's largest country. Pepsi and Coke are both heavily involved in the nation's sport in the way of sponsorship.

Wherever you go in the world – Manchester to Melbourne, Morocco to Malaysia – giant Cola signs beam down at you, street cafés blossom Coke sunshades, T-shirts bear the Pepsi logo. A brown American liquid seems well on its way to fulfilling the New Testament commission to go into all the world and make disciples of all nations.

Universal Culture

At the end of the twentieth century the trappings of 'civilisation' are universal. The icons of the consumer society have crossed the world and are objects of universal adoration. I have a photo from a visit to a poor Arab town in the West Bank area of Israel. Behind the old man saddling his donkey with a sack of cereal are two large billboards – for Coke and Kent cigarettes. On a visit to Morocco I was given a lift by a young Moroccan playing Madonna on his car stereo as we drove past Schweppes and Marlboro adverts. At the 'holy mountain' of Osore-san in Northern Japan, the offerings people leave for the spirits of their ancestors include Ritz crackers and bottles of Coke (the caps removed so the spirits can drink).

The trappings of Western consumerism are sought after everywhere as symbols of progress, status and style, often at the expense of traditional aspects of life in the poorer countries. The Good Life is increasingly defined as the possession of more and more of these consumer goods.

In Northern India the community of Ladakh was cut off from the twentieth century until as recently as 1975. The life-style was one of subsistence farming – just enough to ensure an adequate style of life – and the rest of the time was spent in communal activities, such as storytelling and playing with the children. When a road was built, linking Ladakh with the rest of India and the rest of the world, at least two things happened.

The first was that the Ladakhis realised that compared with the images of life in other parts of India and the world, they were materially poor. The second thing was that they were given a new ideal of what is desirable in life from the media. The Ladakhis began to work hard to make personal profit to spend on consumer goods. Community relationships became secondary to this desire to acquire goods. The tradition of village storytelling all but died out.[1]

The Ladakhis had joined in with the consumer definition of the good life and other values were steamrollered in the process.

Alongside Coke and Pepsi, another major icon of Western lifestyle is the cigarette, particularly Marlboro – the world's best selling brand. By 1980 over 70 billion Marlboro cigarettes were being sold outside America every year. According to Peter Taylor in his book on the politics of tobacco, *The Smoke Ring*, 'The Marlboro cowboys became a symbol that cigarettes made you virile, not sick.' Marlboro's parent company, Philip Morris, sells over 160 brands in more than 170 countries.

Cigarettes are heavily pushed in the developing world through advertising, which reinforces the view that smoking is a sign of style and self-confidence. Dr Ruth Tshabala, of the Public Health unit in Mbabane, Swaziland, reported to the World Health Organisation:

> Among the young, smoking is a sign of maturity, sophistication and freedom. Cigarettes are massively promoted through the press.[2]

Frequently the advertising is through commercials that would never be allowed in the West. Many developing countries do not have the restrictions on portraying smoking as a happy, healthy, glamorous activity, as we do in Britain. In many of these countries, such as Brazil, there are no health warnings on cigarette advertising.

Another US export, rapidly becoming as notorious around the world as Coke and Marlboro, is the hamburger – particularly as made by McDonalds. One new McDonalds burger restaurant opens every seventeen hours somewhere in the world. By 1987 the company had 9,410 outlets serving 19 million people every day. In Asia, McDonalds opens 100 new stores every year.

In America, Ronald McDonald, the clown who appears in the company's advertising and on its stationery in the restaurants, comes second only to Father Christmas in tests to discover who is the best known figure to US children. All over the Macworld, McDonalds Hamburger Universities train budding hamburgerologists in the produce and sale of quality hamburgers.

It is oddly reminiscent of the days of colonialism, when the culture of a larger power was superimposed onto the traditional ways of another. The new colonialism comes not from the barrel of a gun, but from packets, ring-pull cans and the offices of the advertisers.

Development Theory

The arrival of Western consumerism in the developing world stems not just from the marketing strategies of a few sharp-witted companies, but it is bolstered by a whole theory of world development – Modernisation Theory. The theory has it that only by joining in the world system of trade can a country rise to prosperity.

It has its roots in the economics of Adam Smith (1723–90), whose ideas were vital to the rise of capitalism in the West. Smith's emphasis was on progress through self-interest. As an individual pursues his own well-being he necessarily helps the well-being of society at large. As Smith states in *The Wealth of Nations*:

> He (the individual) generally, indeed, neither intends to promote the public interest, nor knows how much he is promoting it... he is in this, as in many other cases, led by an invisible hand to promote an end which was no part of his intention.

In other words, if everybody looks after his own prosperity and his own good, society as a whole will have a larger shared total of prosperity and well-being. Selfishness, far from being condemned, is used to advantage for the individual and society as a whole. This is known as the 'laissez-faire' or 'free market' theory of economics much loved by the Conservative Party and supported by the majority of Western business.

At first the theory was only applied to the West, where it was developed. Then in 1960, it was made popular as a view of how the poor countries of the Third World could develop too – Modernisation Theory. It was expressed by W.W. Rostow, in his 1960 book, *A Non-Communist Manifesto*. He suggested that any country, anywhere in the world, could pass through a series of stages of development. The first stage is 'Underdeveloped', leading up to the final stage, 'High mass consumption'.

Modernisation Theory was widely accepted as the model for development in the 1950s and 1960s, and is still the model favoured by Conservatives and international finance agencies such as the World Bank. However, Modernisation Theory comes loaded with a whole baggage of assumptions.

The first assumption is that this definition of development is the best one. It assumes that progress can be equated with material prosperity. Even the terms 'developed', 'underdeveloped' and 'development' betray this assumption. It says that if a nation has no industry or consumerism and if its people are not prosperous, it is a less successful country. It says the Good Life means having money and the ability to buy consumer goods. It says that a country which is not 'modernised' is failing and implies that a country which has glossy shops, marketing and fat wallets is by definition a better place than a nation of villages and smallholdings.

A second assumption follows from this – that obstacles to this 'progress' should be removed, and it is in the interests of society and individuals to do so. Blocks of this sort might include clinging to your ancestral land rather than moving to where the industry is, in cities, or an over-fondness for your wider family or clan and its traditions. How can a country progress when so much time is taken up with pointless initiation rites, time wasted on storytelling, the elderly, and so on? So we have seen mass movement to the cities of the Third World, and a dramatic weakening of a traditional sense of roots and belonging.

Assumption number three is that if a country fails to develop in this way, it must be the fault of the nation. It is not producing the right goods which people want, its methods are inefficient, its people are lazy. Not, of course, that the whole trading system might be unfair – the developing nation is alone responsible for its own success or failure in development.

Yet all three of these assumptions are highly questionable. They stem from a Westernised, industrialised view of the world and what is right or desirable, and what the meaning of life itself is. It is a theory designed to pat the developed nations on the back and allow them to sit back comfortably – they have made it, they have a duty to enlighten the poor of the world, and if the poor don't manage it, it must be their own fault.

We need to look at each of these assumptions in more depth, along with their value-system that Western equals good, traditional equals bad. But first, we can consider one area where this patently hasn't been the case – diet. We now have a vast body of evidence that as people in the developing world have adopted Western lifestyles, they have also developed Western illnesses.

Western Diet

In traditional societies, such as Africa, heart disease was virtually unknown. In recent years, the consumption of Western foods, which are high in fat and sugar, has made heart disease a new problem in the Third World which never existed before. A meeting of the World Health Organisation in Geneva, in June 1988, referred to Western foods and tobacco as a 'deadly combination'. It was reported at the WHO meeting that over thirty per cent of workers in Sao Paulo, Brazil – home of the Cola Wars – were found to have high blood pressure. The WHO stated that if the current trend continues, by the year 2000 no less than fifteen to twenty per cent of all deaths in the Third World will be due to heart disease.

Despite efforts by the fast food chains to persuade consumers that their food is nutritionally sound, it is generally accepted in medical circles that in fact it is low in food value. The differences between Western diet and traditional diets of the Third World have been highlighted in *Fibre Man*, the fascinating life story of Dr Denis Burkitt, the man primarily responsible for discovering the need for fibre in the diet.

The book contains the text of a lecture he gave in Doncaster in 1984, which includes Dr Burkitt's discoveries about diabetes and other diseases:

> To give you an idea of how lifestyle can alter diabetes, there is a little island in the Pacific called Nauru.... In 1952 its people had a very low level of diabetes just as most other Pacific islanders have. Then it was found that the island was covered with phosphates. The islanders sold their phosphate and became the second richest people in the world next to the oil-rich Arabs.
>
> They began looking at glossy magazines and saw what clever people the Americans and English were, with their hi-fi sets, radios and cars. They came to the erroneous conclusion that we knew what was best to eat. So they gave up their local food, changed to a more Western lifestyle and grossly over-ate. Now forty per cent of the island's population over the age of twenty is diabetic and obesity is rampant.
>
> They have also learned how to get appendicitis; that starts early. They won't develop coronary heart disease or gall-stones for another twenty years, but they will come.[3]

Burkitt explains that obesity is a problem of the modern Western world. It has not even been a large problem in Western history until recently. Cromwell had an army of 40,000 and literature records that none of them were fat. Burkitt found that as well as the excessive use of fats and sugars in the Western diet, the absence of rough dietary fibre which is refined away in the West meant people were left more vulnerable to food-related illnesses of many types. Compared with 1946, twice as many British children are now obese and have eczema, six times as many have diabetes and three times as many have asthma.

There is a similar pattern in cigarette-related illness and death. Peter Taylor records how a professor of medicine at the University of Sao Paulo told him that over the past forty years, lung cancer deaths in the state of Sao Paulo had nearly trebled amongst men aged forty to forty-five, gone up nearly seven times in men aged fifty to fifty-nine and nearly nine times in men aged sixty to sixty-nine. The doctor blamed the rise on 'the massive advertising on television which associates cigarettes with glamour and success in life.[4]

Individualism

Modernisation theory comes from a set of assumptions about what matters in a society, and what people should be aiming to achieve in life. It shares the usual Western assumption that a human's personal development is one towards independence and self-sufficiency. We are sent away from home to go to school, we are trained for economic self-reliance. We are constantly told we will need to stand on our own two feet. We look towards the day when we 'fly the nest' and gain our own income. We leave to get married. And even when we are unemployed, Social Security enables us to maintain economic independence (although even then, many of us are reluctant to accept 'hand outs' because it implies we cannot stand on those two feet). My identity resides in what I *do* – it says something about me – and what I *have* – it makes me feel I am somebody.

On the other hand the African mind has, until recently, had an entirely different set of assumptions about what matters most and about the point of life. The African identity is rooted in family and community, with a particular emphasis on the wider family. This too has been embodied in the system of education used. Education is geared not towards independence, but dependence. You are taught about family history, the family land, how to conduct personal relationships with those around you. Education itself is carried out inside the home.

The former President of Kenya, Jomo Kenyatta, has written about the traditions and world-view of his own tribe, the Gikuyu:

The striking thing in the Gikuyu system of education, and the feature which most sharply distinguishes it from the European system of education, is the primary place given to personal relationships.... While the Westerner asserts that character formation is the chief thing, he forgets that character is formed primarily through relations with other people, and that there is really no other way in which it can grow. Europeans assume that, given the right knowledge and ideas, personal relations can be left largely to take care of themselves, and this is perhaps the most fundamental difference in outlook between Africans and Europeans.'[5]

At the time of initiation of a Gikuyu youth into adulthood, there is a teaching period of several months, in which there is a special focus on how to relate to one's future in-laws. In traditional African society, weddings frequently have more than 400 people involved, and a feature of Kenyan tradition is the Harambee – which means 'let's all pull together'. Everybody in the neighbourhood downs tools and comes round to lend a hand with the task you're involved in.

In the West, the nuclear family is the accepted model of the family. But in the majority of countries of the world, including almost all developing countries, have preferred the wider family pattern, because of the sense of support and roots which it can provide. As in the genealogies of the Old and New Testaments, an African's identity is seen in relation to his wider relatives.

But with the coming of Westernisation there has been a drift to the cities and fragmentation of the family unit. Such is the predicament of the traditional African family that a Kenyan, Bedan Mbugua, has formed the African Family Development Trust to fight to save the family. The Trust has its headquarters in the Kenyan capital, Nairobi, and employs a full-time staff of seven. Bedan told me he believes the loss of the old patterns of family may be more serious than most people think:

With the coming of the Western capitalist system and the ethic of keeping what you earn for yourself, the tradition of sharing all you have with the family may soon be lost. We in the Trust are working for a society where the care between people is used as a measure of our development, not just economics. Development has had good points, but we in Africa are now starting to evaluate whether development could have taken place without sacrificing relationships. Development should not be lop-sided.

According to Bedan, Western assumptions about independence are inadequate: 'Self-reliance is in the end an illusion. People always need to be loved and cared for. They can never exist on their own. People cannot ultimately be satisfied with independence. The Western ideology of independence can mean denying oneself the best source of love and care. In a sense, it is cutting off your nose to spite your face!'

Individualism is also a severing of the major counterbalance to the messages of the Western desire-makers. The individual is vulnerable, battered on all sides by the images and messages of consumerism – in the West and developing countries alike. Family, community, religious faith all give a wider reference point for assessing the messages. They are the spanner of reality in the dream machine, the open window which allows daylight into the private, secretive room of our individualised fantasies and ambitions.

Kenyatta writes that in Gikuyu tradition, individualism is associated with black magic. Lucy Irvine, author of *Castaway*, tells how the natives of the island where she lived had thought sailors must be devils. Who else, they reasoned, would have willingly cut themselves off from family, roots and land to wander the face of the earth?

A friend told me that a Pakistani boy in her children's Cambridge school was being taunted by other schoolboys. In anger, he summoned the worst insult he could think of: 'Your mother is a donkey!' He was shocked when the other children just chuckled. In the society he had been brought up in, to insult members of another's family is the worst possible slight.

Wider Family

Your presuppositions colour the way you view a whole range of things. One of these is the question of the elderly. In a consumer society, where people are defined largely in relation to their capacities as producers and consumers of goods, there is little place for an unproductive seventy-year-old. The elderly are left at the margins of life and culture, put in homes out of sight. We increasingly talk about the 'problem of the elderly' as the average age of the population grows.

In a survey of a Cambridge geriatric ward, the pro-family group Familybase found that out of seventy-two people in the ward, forty-two of them never received a visitor. In an Age Concern study of 1974, eighty-two per cent of old people questioned said the worst problem facing them was loneliness. In general, the elderly are not so much valued as tolerated.

However, in the so-called underdeveloped countries, old people are not seen as elderly but as 'elders'. Age is associated with wisdom and experience, unlike the West, where age is associated with being out of touch with modern life. Grandparents are an integral part of the family, constantly on hand and playing a key role in educating children. A strong extended family group means people rarely feel the sense of rootlessness and alienation which gnaws at so many in the developed world. As Bedan Mbugua told me, the process of development and learning applies at least as much to the West as to the Third World:

> We in Africa are rich in the area of relationships. We have been receiving the technology which Africa needs to develop, but we should also be able to offer that which we have – the warmth and care of the family. Without this, human beings are incomplete.

Bedan's comments strike at the heart of our system of

priorities, not only as a nation but as individuals. How highly do we value relationships, and what steps are we prepared to take to strengthen them?

When Derbyshire draftsman Stephen Hartle drew up plans for a family party it wasn't just for his own immediate family plus Granny. He brought together 150 members of his wider family for a huge family reunion in a big hall near his home in the Pennines. The ages of family members who attended ranged from two to eighty-four, and people travelled from as far afield as London to share family memories and meet new faces. The centrepiece of the event was a large family cake. Mr Hartle, aged forty-two, said the aim of the party was to strengthen ties because of the happy memories he had of family events in his own childhood:

> My father Joe loved family gatherings and socialised within the family a great deal. It was a large, close-knit family. So I grew up surrounded by uncles, aunts and cousins. We really enjoyed the close family contact and never saw it as anything but a benefit and a pleasure. I'm very thankful for what my father and his brothers and sisters put into the family, and it's sad to see that go. The time is rapidly coming when that generation won't be with us, and the younger members now live quite a distance apart. Family ties are tending to disappear. The family unit is being undermined these days, but for me it has been a real source of happiness and security. It is too valuable to let it disappear.

Perhaps the place where all of us can start working at relationships is in the small things. Mealtimes can be a time for conversation instead of a silent munch in front of the TV. We can make time to listen to those around us, or ask how somebody is feeling. We can get round to writing that letter to Granny.

Roots and Land

Another area in which we can see our world-view at work is in land. For Westerners land is a commodity to be bought and sold. In Britain today, property (along with the land it stands on) is the single biggest financial asset. Because land tends to have no deeper meaning or significance to us, we have a high rate of job mobility.

It has been said that IBM stands for, 'I've been moved!' Like many other companies, the large computer manufacturer is reputed to have a personnel policy which often involves high job mobility for its employees. The company is not unusual in this. Tax inspectors are regularly moved as a matter of course, as are the military, bank managers, diplomats, junior doctors and trainee managers of department stores. Some Civil Service departments can look like a nationwide game of musical chairs because of job mobility.

This is not accidental. It stems from a certain, low view of the importance of land, belonging and roots. Mobility has widely been seen as a positive thing. It implies progress, opportunity, promotion, new horizons. Less thought, as many Africans would tell you, is given to the problems it can bring to relationships, particularly those in the family.

The US Army conducted an inquiry into the high divorce rates among its members. Divorce and other social problems were found frequently to be the result of the constant uprooting of couples and families. The Army adopted a policy of lower mobility. The Army's findings are confirmed by academic research. A 1976 study concluded that job mobility was 'a recurring feature of marriage breakdown'.

An explanation of this has been offered by Rev Bruce Winter, Warden of Tyndale House in Cambridge. He is an Anglican minister with wide experience of the problems brought about by mobility. For many years he was vicar of St George's Church, Singapore, a church attended by many diplomats and business people on short-term assignments:

The mobile man tends to be married to his company. He works long hours and gets a sense of identity from his work. But what about his wife's identity? Most of the British wives in Singapore were housewives who had been part of a network of friends and neighbours back home. When they were uprooted, the marriage alone had to sustain an identity which had been rooted in a wider community. Often it could not take the pressure.

Carefully built credentials and a sense of knowing and being known by a group were hard to transfer. After the second or third move, some wives stopped trying to adapt altogether. Many felt anonymous and inadequate. As an Australian, Bruce Winter said this isolation was often aggravated by traditional British reserve: 'Stress and loneliness are bottled up until a wife can't cope any more and she takes to the bottle or tranquillisers.'

The problem is not exclusive to travellers. A health visitor in a prosperous Midlands town once commented to a friend of mine that the most acutely depressed people she knew were the mobile, wealthy residents of the new housing estates. One of the West's biggest – and least acknowledged – problems is the inner emptiness which stems from a lack of intimacy, a lack of people who know you and are on hand to help, support and offer a shoulder to cry on. According to *New Internationalist* magazine, three of every five women who stay at home to look after small children are on tranquillisers such as Valium.

Among the areas in the UK with the highest rates of suicide is its newest town, Milton Keynes. Can it be a coincidence that these deaths are happening in the most rootless place in these isles? The people of Milton Keynes are people uprooted from other regions and communities and dropped together, then expected to grow new roots instantly.

A second form of job mobility in the West today is that forced on people by regional decline. It is encouraged by the political theory which says that if there are no jobs in your region, you should travel to where the work is. As Norman Tebbitt told the 1981 Conservative Party Conference, you should get 'on your bike!' However, another leading politician, Labour frontbencher Donald Anderson, has no doubt about the effects such policies have on relationships: 'My own father left my home in South Wales to seek work in the West country, leaving his family behind. The movement of people to look for work outside their family areas is a major element in the breakdown of families.'

Mobility means that members of the wider family, especially the elderly, are left behind. The social consequences of this can be serious. Over a million elderly people have no regular visitors. Care which might have been given by family members falls by necessity to the state. Grandparents have less frequent access to grandchildren and vice versa.

A more general consequence is that society places less emphasis on roots and belonging. The self-realisation of the individual is pursued at the expense of family and community. It is an attitude which can leave a toll of broken marriages, elderly people with no family contact and children growing up without a sense of community.

It would be impractical and undesirable to try to eliminate all mobility. For most of us there is a time when, as the old gospel song has it, 'When the good Lord calls, I gotta move!' Some moving of jobs may be good and necessary. But the real issue is this: is it desirable that government and private companies should encourage enforced mobility? A society which had as a priority the building of strong family and community relationships has good reasons for saying no.

There are societies which have said no, ones with a different world-view from that of our Western consumer culture. As Kenyatta explains, the identity of his own tribe is closely bound up with the land:

> In studying the Gikuyu tribal organisation it is necessary to take into consideration land tenure as the most important factor in the social, political religious and economic life of the tribe.... Among the Gikuyu the soil is especially honoured, and an everlasting oath is to swear by the earth.'[6]

Because land in Gikuyu society is family-owned, it also

binds together relationships. So much is the land bound up in identity that there is no free market for land. Land is the 'mother' of the tribe and who would lightly sell their own mother? If a man wanted to buy another's land he would brew a beer, take it to his neighbour and the men would speak using the language of courtship and marriage. If the seller agreed they would join in a ceremony of boundary-marking, after which they see each other as in-laws.

As Kenyatta explains, 'When the European comes to the Gikuyu country and robs the people of their land, he is taking away not only their livelihood, but the material symbol that holds family and tribe together.'[7]

The arrival of Westernisation has meant that this traditional rootedness in the land is breaking down. Bedan Mbugua explained:

> The majority of Africans still live in extended family groups. But increasing Westernisation has put a strain on the structures. People drift to the cities, where things are designed to favour the nuclear family, as opposed to the wider family. Houses are built for small families. Taxation and benefits are all worked out on a nuclear family model.

Love of the land is not something exclusive to the Third World. When I interviewed Callum MacDonald, songwriter of the Scottish rock group Runrig, he told me the landscape of the band's native Skye had a profound influence on his own songwriting:

> The importance of roots and belonging is very great. If you were to ask about the common theme in our writing, I'd say it was the land – a sense of its past and the people who've been through that landscape. You can't help but be influenced by landscape if you live somewhere like Skye. You're surrounded by mountains all around. The songs are about the spiritual dimension of roots and belonging to the landscape, its history, people and the Gaelic language.

Consequently, it is not only mountains, crags and sky which are prominent themes in Runrig's songs, but also land ownership and social justice. The very name Runrig is a form of land tenure in the Outer Hebrides.

The song *The Cutter*, from the band's recent album, *The Cutter and the Clan*, underlines the theme:

> It's about a friend of mine who emigrated from the Outer Hebrides in the 1960s and moved to Canada. He left Scotland penniless, but when he reached Canada he worked his way up until he was head of his own company. It's a real rags-to-riches story, and he's now extremely wealthy. But he still comes back to the Outer Hebrides to cut the peat for his ageing mother. It's a kind of ritual he has to do every year. For him, all that he's achieved doesn't mean the same as what he's left behind.

As for the rest of us, most of us rarely seem to notice what we've left behind. We rarely make the link between the loneliness and isolation around us and in our own lives and our world-view which places belonging – both to other people and to a place – so low on its list of priorities. The main reason given by businessmen for refusing relocation to another part of the country or world is family ties. Yet most seem to have swallowed a world-view which places personal affluence and status above all else. Maybe we should take a scrap of paper, note down all the dimensions of our lives – family, job, hobbies, faith, entertainment and others – and then ask ourselves which of them actually matters.

When colonial powers went to poor nations they took with them the Western world-view, which coloured their view of the supposedly primitive cultures they colonised. Time and again we see cultures whose insights on areas such as family, land and nature were not so much respected as trampled: the North American Indians, the Aborigines of Australia, the traditional patterns of African society. As violent as the clash of weapons was the clash of world-views between the Western settlers and native peoples.

Of course it would be naive to claim that Westernisation and modernisation have not had a positive side for many poor countries. Infant mortality has been reduced, health care improved, new forms of education made more widespread, life is more comfortable. Some technology has helped with the digging of wells, irrigation and the development of new strains of rice, and so on. When the United Fruit Company went to Central America in the late nineteenth century, they built up a local transport network and many of the advantages of American life, which brought benefits to locals as well as the company. Today, too, many transnationals contribute to the local health care and education of their host countries.

It would be wrong to adopt the stance of the Jewish zealot in the Monty Python film, *The Life of Brian*, who indignantly asked what good the Romans had done for Palestine, only to be met with a chorus of replies from those around him, including references to roads, drainage and law and order. The picture is far from one-sided.

But Bedan Mbugua's underlying unease remains. Is a 'development' not possible which respects a world-view other than that of selfish Western consumerism? Is development not possible without destroying much of that which is most valuable in human terms? With the notable exception of E F Schumacher's Intermediate Technology Development Group, recent history is sadly lacking in good examples of a model of development which offers a radical alternative to the Western-assumption-based Modernisation Theory.

Unequal Trade

The other area which Modernisation Theory assumes about free trade between developed and underdeveloped countries is that it really is free. It invites the Third World to join in the West's consumer party and become developed, on the understanding that it will stand a sporting chance of achieving this.

For some, this has happened: South Korea, Singapore and Taiwan have become successful exporters of TVs, computers and hi-fi equipment to the West. But others have grown poorer. According to the Paris-based Organisation for Economic Cooperation and Development (OECD), in 1988 the gap between rich and poor nations was wider than it had been ten years earlier. Is this the fault of the poor countries, or have they in fact been invited to play with loaded dice? According to Modernisation Theory, underdevelopment is the first step towards development. According to another theory of development, Dependency Theory, poverty is actually *caused* by development in other parts of the world.

Dependency Theory is the picture of development favoured by relief agencies, such as Oxfam, TEAR Fund and Christian Aid. It says it is inaccurate to compare the rise of modern Third World nations with the early stages of capitalist development in, for example, Britain. For one, Britain had no competitors in international trade at that stage. Now, Third World nations have to compete in a massive global system of trade with its own rules already set. Supporters of Dependency Theory point out that 1955–75 saw the greatest economic growth the world has ever seen, but it was also the time when the gap between the rich and poor countries grew more than ever before. Clearly the poor were not benefitting from the growth of the wealthy nations.

The report of the Brandt Commission in 1980 predicted that by the year 2000, we are likely to see twice as many poor people in the world as there were when the report was written.[8]

One reason for the imbalance is the power of Western advertising. Desires and 'needs' in developing countries are being re-educated by the all-pervasive media so that Big Macs are preferred to local foods, Coke preferred to the locally-produced drink, Western clothes to local dress. Home-produced goods, usually less glamorous, but more profitable for the local economy, can't hope to compete against the big bucks of the Western desire-makers.

Transnational Companies

Another reason for trade imbalance is the people who pull the strings of international trade. Most of the food exported from the developing countries is controlled by large, Western-owned transnational companies. Of the 100 largest economic powers in the world fifty-seven are countries. The remaining forty-three are transnationals. The major companies control forty per cent of the world's trade and ninety per cent of trade in raw commodities, such as coffee, tea and sugar and minerals. In 1985, the sales of US tobacco giant Philip Morris (owners of Marlboro) were more than the Gross Domestic Product of Kenya.

Because of their size the transnationals have a great influence over the terms of trade. One of these, Unilever, controls eighty per cent of the international seed market and ninety-five per cent of India's packet tea trade. It makes a massive contribution to the economies of developing countries and, as such, wields great influence over the governments of these countries.

Not being tied to any single country, transnationals can move to wherever labour is cheapest. This has resulted in companies shifting – or threatening to shift – from one continent to another at the drop of a hat. One country is played off against another. Because all developing countries are desperate for business, they each offer concessions, such as tax exemptions to the transnationals to make sure they don't pull out and take their trade with them. That way the profit to the developing countries themselves is kept to a minimum.

This causes another problem for the producing country. The instability this causes makes it hard to plan long term. You don't know if the company will be buying your sugar, tea or seed next year.

Because transnationals own much of the agricultural land in the developing world, it frequently results in the ironic situation of the best land, which could be cultivated for local food needs, being used to produce crops for rich consumer countries. The Third World land under cultivation for export produce increased eleven per cent between 1974 and 1984.

Transnationals argue that in a world of food shortages, large-scale plantations are the only way to grow enough to feed everybody. But needs being met are not so much those of locals but those of Westerners for between-meal snacks. Even if more is produced, no more necessarily goes to those in need.

The companies not only sell most of the food bought from the Third World. They also ship, process and package the goods, so that it is they and not the producer country who reaps most of the profits from the sales of the goods. It is estimated that just 11.5 per cent of the retail price of bananas gets back to the countries which produce them.

According to Oxfam's John Clark, home-processing would dramatically increase profits for producer countries: 'The 50 poorest countries could double their export earnings if they could process their commodities and export cocoa powder rather than beans, instant coffee rather than beans for example.'[19]

But when Third World countries decide to go it alone and process, ship and package their own goods, they often find trade barriers from the Western governments which limit the goods of this kind which can enter the country. This process is known as protectionism and is particularly true of textiles.

Imports of clothing and textiles into developed countries is regulated by the 'Multi-Fibre Arrangement' (MFA). The MFA sets strict limits on the quantities which can be imported from developing countries. Western countries can trade freely. Groups such as the World Development Movement are calling on governments to allow freer trade with the West.

The claim that this would result in massive job losses in the West is described as an exaggeration by Philip Cole, EEC Campaigns Officer of the WDM:

> It would be wrong to claim that no jobs have been lost by competition from the developing countries but why should they be the only ones discriminated against? Other industrialised countries account for 70 per cent of Britain's imports of textiles and clothing, developing countries for only 28 per cent. Studies in recent years have calculated that half of all British job losses in textiles and clothing are due to new technology. Of the job losses caused by increased imports, only one third were due to competition from developing countries.[28]

Philip Cole believes justice and mercy demand that profits back home should not be the only rules governing international trade, because this inevitably results in discrimination against the poorest peoples of the world.

Because of the restrictions on processed goods, many developing countries become dependent on a raw commodity for export. In 1984, 88 per cent of Zambia's export income was from copper, 50 per cent of Sudan's from cotton, and 59 per cent of Bangladesh's from jute. This means they become vulnerable to the ups and downs of the international marketplace for these commodities. As the price of commodities gradually falls, the developing countries have to keep on producing more and more for export just to stand still.

So is the answer for developing countries simply to pull out of international trade? Oxfam's John Clark suggests this would not be a lasting solution. Rather, he puts forward areas where Western governments can work to make sure the trade conditions for the developing world are less weighted against the poor:

▷ Assist the cooperation between developing countries in improving their own trade opportunities.

▷ Reduce the barriers to imports from the Third World

especially in the case of the poorest countries.

▷ Support international efforts to impose ethical controls on international companies and commodity speculators.

▷ Support international efforts to stabilise the prices of commodities on which developing countries depend.[11]

And groups such as Traidcraft and TEAR Craft are working to embody a new, ethical form of trade with developing countries. Before entering into trade agreements these groups ensure that workers are paid a good living wage and that the majority of the profits from sales go to the producers and not some Western middle-men. They also embody a new ideal of trade because their trade is based on relationships. Traidcraft workers work closely with producers they know well.

By re-educating our buying habits to include products from groups such as Traidcraft – food, clothing, ornaments, paper and jewellery – each one of us can do a little to encourage fair trade for the poor.

But fair trade is only half the problem. The other half, as Bedan Mbugua points out, is for the developing world to develop without losing the relationships and communities which make people truly human. And for us in the affluent West to look to the traditional societies of the poor countries of the globe and ask if it is us or them who can truly describe ourselves as 'developed'.

Notes

[1] Full story in *Resurgence* No 110, 1985.
[2] Quoted in Peter Taylor, *The Smoke Ring* (Sphere: London, 1985).
[3] Brian Kellock, *Fibre Man, The Life Story of Dr Denis Burkitt* (Lion: Tring, 1985).
[4] Peter Taylor, op cit.

[5] Jomo Kenyatta, *Facing Mount Kenya* (Heinemann Educational: Nairobi, 1978).

[6] *Ibid.*

[7] *Ibid.*

[8] Independent Commission on International Development Issues, *North-South: A Programme for Survival* (Pan: London, 1981).

[9] John Clark, *For Richer for Poorer* (Oxfam: Oxford, 1986).

[10] Philip Cole, 'Protectionism', *Traidcraft Exchange Magazine*, Spring 1987.

[11] John Clark, *op cit.*

10

BORN TO SHOP

The Consumer World-View

Looking at World-Views

It's not unusual to see pictures of the earth. Images of the globe confront us regularly in adverts for airlines, ecological issues, telecommunications companies, computers and in the graphics for news broadcasts. What we are less used to analysing is our own *world-view*, a term I have used from time to time in this book without really explaining it.

A world-view is a person's framework for understanding the world around them. Without a framework, the outside world would simply be a jumble of disconnected objects. A world-view helps you sift which of all the elements in the world matter most, and which apply to your life. It is your way of imposing an order onto randomness. It gives you your moral framework – guidelines and rules for what you should and shouldn't do.

This might sound suspiciously like a definition of religion. Is it? The answer is yes and no. If by religion we mean a way of analysing the whole of life, then yes a world-view is a

religion. But few people in the West do have that understanding of religion. Westerners usually split off the 'religious' into
a separate, watertight realm which only occasionally touches
on the rest of life. The 'sacred' and 'secular' are different
boxes, into which we drop different parts of our lives.

We put into the sacred box our visits to a church – on Sundays, or just for Christmas, Easter and cousin Sue's wedding.
Into the box we also put our occasional prayers, offered in
moments of panic, and our conversations with the local vicar.
Meanwhile 'real life' – work, leisure, watching TV, sex – continue in the other, 'secular' box. After all, what is religious
about cooking or kissing?

Since most of us keep the sacred and secular in separate
boxes, our declared religion can be at odds with our actual
world-view (our framework for the whole of life). So a
businessman may feel no contradiction that he goes to church
on Sunday and encourages somebody to take on an excessive
loan on Monday. Or a student might say she is a Christian but
the assumptions and theories she uses to study philosophy, literature or economics may be in direct contradiction to Christian assumptions governing these areas. We are used to dividing up our lives into boxes in this way, as if different laws
applied to the sacred and secular.

But a world-view does not allow for such dualism between
what you say and what you do, or what you say on Sunday and
do for the rest of the week. Your world-view is the (often
unconscious) set of principles which actually motivate your
every attitude and action. It is a 'holistic' framework, covering
the whole of life.

The Consumer World-View

The most common world-view in the West today is consumerism. Even when we are not aware of it, it seeps in
through our TV, chats in the pub, the paper, adverts. It is in

the very air we breathe. I have written earlier of advertisements and film stars as icons of our culture. A quick look at some more of our cultural icons might help us understand the world-view of consumerism:

▷ *The net curtain (individualism)*. I have my little patch of suburbia which nobody else can claim as theirs. I live my private life behind the curtain and, though I come out occasionally to say hello and lend you my lawn-mower, I pursue my own self-interest above all else. Life is a jungle where only the strongest survive, so you've got to learn to stand on your own two feet. I look after myself because nobody else will.

▷ *The wallet (prosperity)*. Happiness comes through having the good things in life. My dream is one day to win the pools.

▷ *The new car (success)*. I'm somebody who's made it in life. People look up to me; they know I'm somebody who matters.

▷ *The supermarket shelf (freedom of choice)*. I like to choose the things which suit me best – the cans of soup, the church, the school, where I live, the car I drive. I have a right to choose my own way of life.

▷ *The credit card (instant gratification)*. Why should I have to wait? I want the same new gadgets as the next-door neighbours and I want them today.

Most of us accept most of these statements about life as being basically true, because in our consumer society they form a large part of our world-view. It is the world-view we share with most of our neighbours, friends and family. The assumptions are so much a part of us we have problems placing where we got them from. Most of us rarely question the world-view, and have problems seeing it as a world-view because it is so much a part of us. We unconsciously accept much of what we are told and do not question its truth.

I recently discovered that gorillas are placid, vegetarian animals who are mild-tempered and affectionate. Chimpanzees, on the other hand, can be very savage and have been known to tear limbs off humans. I was surprised and at first found this hard to believe. I suppose this was due to watching the antics of PG Tips chimps on adverts and seeing the gorilla King Kong terrorise New York. I uncritically accepted the images I had been fed.

One day my wife and a friend were walking in a park when they heard some birds making a gentle 'hoo… hoo…' sound. The friend said to my wife, 'Oh, just listen to the cuckoos!' My wife, knowing a little more about birds, told her that they were in fact wood pigeons. At first the friend would not believe her. Then my wife asked why she thought they were cuckoos. It turned out that the friend had walked in parks with her uncle as a small girl and the uncle had always said 'Listen to the cuckoos!' when they heard the birds' call. She had never questioned whether it was in fact cuckoos at all. And she had been wrong all this time. She even had emotional reasons (the memory of her uncle) for sticking to her assumption that the birds were cuckoos.

In the words of Dr Johnson, 'Most of us catch our opinions by contagion'. We absorb the opinions floating in the culture round us and make them our own, without examining them critically. The claim of this book is that the consumer worldview, the one most of us have unconsciously absorbed, is an inadequate one. In the words of the late economist E F Schumacher, 'A man who uses an imaginary map, thinking it a true one, is likely to be worse off than someone with no map at all.'[1] But we have our map, consumerism, which deeply affects the way we approach life's biggest issues, such as religion, politics and morality.

Religion

Prosperity Theology

The most recent trend in American evangelical theology (and the evangelicals are the largest Christian group in America, with around one third of Americans claiming to be 'born again') has been dubbed the 'health and wealth' gospel. The idea starts with the totally orthodox assertion that Christianity is not just an 'other-worldly' faith, that material goods are entirely positive in themselves because God looked at his creation and declared it 'very good'.

The next step in prosperity logic is that because God is a loving father he cannot possibly countenance his children going without and that poverty is therefore a result of sin – or, at least, lack of faith. Likewise, bad health is caused by faithlessness and your healing simply has to be 'claimed' from the Lord. God is a heavenly banker who guarantees a massive return on whatever you give for his work on earth. 'You sow it, God will grow it,' says Oral Roberts the TV evangelist, best remembered for his claim that God would 'call him home' unless viewers sent in $8m to his Oklahoma headquarters. 'Name it and claim it' say a bevy of of other evangelists. Kenneth Copeland, a well known preacher from Texas, has produced a video, *Power to Prosper*, which is regularly shown in the UK as well as across the US. His wife Gloria penned the book *God's Will is to Prosper*.

If wealth is a sign of God's favour, little surprise that many of the prosperity evangelists feel no contradiction in living in luxury homes and owning executive jets. Nor do their followers question the evangelists' right to the wealth. After all, they reason, don't a range of Old Testament texts equate prosperity and blessing?

The result is a Christianity which bears an uncanny similarity to the American Dream. The author Andrew Brandon has made a study of prosperity theology and argues:

> The health and wealth gospel has all the colour and flare of a TV commercial. It is perfectly adapted to the obsessions of men and women in the latter part of the twentieth century.[2]

Perhaps the ultimate example of this pandering to the spirit of the age is the drive-in church. Like 'sex-shop', 'drive-in church' ought to be a contradiction in terms. Church should be about relationship: an opening up to God and to others. But there they are, springing up across America, the logical consequence of a generation whose goals are privacy and self-fulfilment.

Of course, it does not necessarily follow that because the church is taking on board ideas from the world these ideas are corrupting it. In recent years it has been challenged from outside on a range of issues, such as the role of women and care for the environment, and has been moved to take up what many see as a more biblical stance on the issues. But prosperity theology is different. It is at odds with the heart of the orthodox gospel. In the words of Andrew Brandon,

> They've taken Jesus to a cosmetic surgeon for a face-lift. His profile and message do not fit our materialistic world, so we conveniently change them... The rich young ruler can keep his money; the 'eye of the needle' has been enlarged by a major building contractor; the poor are no longer blessed but the rich inherit the earth.[3]

Prosperity theology is the point at which God and mammon shake hands and realise they have been on the same side all along.

The Wider Church

Even many Christians who do not accept prosperity theology have taken on board much of the consumer world-view into their faith. We have largely privatised religion, so its starting point is *my* self-fulfilment. God, instead of threatening our self-interest, legitimises it. Our evangelism tells people Jesus will make them happy and fulfilled. Jesus is *my* saviour and the hymns I sing are about *my personal* relationship with God. Prayer can become a 'shopping list' of requests, rather than experiencing a profound relationship with the creator. Conversion is 'making a decision for Christ', rather than a response to God's call, salvation is by faith (mine) rather than grace (God's). And so often we talk about taking a 'collection' (getting) rather than an 'offertory' (giving).

The *Reader's Digest Abridged Bible* only does what most Western Christians already do with regard to Scripture: pick out their favourite bits and leave the rest on one side. Similarly, we have privatised our conception of sin so it only refers to private sexuality and personal habits rather than wider issues of justice, oppression and materialism. We have reduced a transforming vision for the whole of life to a private hobby and an individualised set of rules.

The result is that we have so focused on a narrow range of wood chips that we have missed some planks. In the words of Mike Yaconelli, editor of the satirical American religious magazine, *The Wittenburg Door*, most Christians have swallowed the individualistic consumer world-view: 'I am afraid that we have been so concerned with pornography, with drugs and alcohol, with abortion that, in our passion to face these issues, we have allowed even worse demons to slip in the back door and become part of the landscape.'[4]

Many Christians have reversed Christ's injunction to be '*in* the world but not *of* it', so that they are *of* the world (they share its basic world-view), but not *in* it (they like to stand aloof and show themselves to be set apart and not 'worldly'). They have become consumerised.

Pick'n'Mix Religion

Many of us like to pick'n'mix our religion as we select sweets at Woolworths.

Because in the modern mind the heart of religion is *my* self-fulfilment rather than the irresistible tug of an almighty God, it becomes legitimate to concoct a spirituality to meet my needs as I see them. Many people who call themselves Christians hold to a 'fundamentalist liberalism' which holds up tolerance, open-mindedness and self-fulfilment as ultimates. They stubbornly see orthodox Christians as simple or naive, refusing to accept that a thinking person can submit himself or herself to the God of the Bible, with his exclusive claims and rigorous demands.

If somebody insists that there is a universal truth which applies to all people in all cultures they are told, 'Yes, dear, that's fine for you but not for me.' Such people hold up relativism as an absolute, impervious to the charge of the American rock singer Steve Taylor that they are 'So open minded that their brains leaked out'.[5]

The 1960s were an age of pick'n'mix religion. Many Westerners, following in the wake of the Beatles, experienced a crisis of faith in consumerism as they realised that material goods could not satisfy spiritual impulses. But they were unwilling to throw out the basic world-view of consumerism and accept orthodox Christian spirituality. Rather, they turned East to gurus and drugs which promised the experiences of religion but without its moral demands. For the 1960s a 'faith' which promised peace of mind, ecstasy, and purpose but didn't challenge your appetite for hallucenogenics or sexual athletics was at the heart of 'alternative' youth consumerism. Today, various forms of Eastern meditation and drug-taking still offer a similar pick'n'mix: 'religious' experience without the moral demands.

The same charge can be made against so-called 'New Age' beliefs (in reality very old fashioned pantheism dressed up in yuppie garb and designer packaging), with all its talk of looking inwards, discovering inner truth and finding the inner light. Early this century G.K. Chesterton was scathing about such claims: 'Of all concievable forms of enlightenment the worst is what... people call the Inner Light. Of all horrible religions the most horrible is the God within.'

Chesterton explains that the philosophy is actually no more than good old pagan selfishness, disguised by religious-sounding language. The very point of Christianity is to assert forcefully that navel-gazing (even at the most illuminated navel) is an inadequate way to find the deepest truths about life, meaning and God:

> That Jones shall worship the god within him turns out ultimately to mean that Jones shall worship Jones... Christianity came into the world firstly to assert with violence that a man had not only to look inwards, but to look outwards, to behold with astonishment and enthusiasm a divine company and a divine captain. The only fun of being a Christian was that a man was not left alone with the Inner Light, but definitely recognised an outer light...'[6]

Our consignment of religion to being a 'private matter' goes some way to explain the discrepancy in UK church attendance: in an Independent Broadcasting Authority survey (December 1988) on religious belief in Britain, 74 per cent said they believed Jesus Christ was the Son of God. But less than 10 per cent actually attend church services. Religion is a private affair, alongside toilets and contraceptives in the list of things you are not public about. If this attitude was expressed as a small ad in a paper it might read:

> Journalist, 26, seeks warm, caring divinity for occasional fun at Christmas, Easter and Remembrance Day. No ties or commitment.

The problem with pick'n'mix religion is that it shares the sheer arrogance of all consumerism: I am all that matters, my fulfilment is supreme. It reduces God to a consumer disposable which can be picked up and dropped at will. Contrary to the biblical claim that God is truth, whether we like it or not, and we need to adapt ourselves to the truth, we say *we* are central and truth must adapt to suit our wishes. Pick'n'mix belief sets the individual above all the great world religions, somehow able to select the bits he likes the look of and reject the rest. He is the source of all knowledge, able to make unfounded generalisations such as 'they are all the same really', 'they are just different ways of climbing the same mountain'.

C S Lewis reminds us that there is a time when we have to stop picking'n'mixing our religion and acknowledge a higher power in the universe than *me*:

> There comes a moment when the children who have been playing at burglars hush suddenly: was that a *real* footstep in the hall? There comes a moment when people who have been dabbling in religion ('Man's search for God'!) suddenly draw back. Supposing we really found Him? We never meant it to come to *that*! Worse still, supposing He had found us?[7]

Politics

The New Right

The political embodiment of the consumer world-view is seen *par excellence* in the 'New Right', known more colloquially as Thatcherism, Reaganomics, or hard-line capitalism. The New Right holds up material prosperity, individualism, success and freedom of choice to be ultimates. These are the goals to which politics must aspire.

The economic vision of the New Right can be traced back to the Scottish economist Adam Smith. Smith's theory, outlined briefly in the previous chapter in connection with world development, was that if each person in society pursues his own self-interest and happiness, then the total 'pool' of happiness and well-being of the nation will rise. As people worked for personal gain, an 'invisible hand' would ensure they also promoted the public good.

Economic life has laws which should be allowed to run unimpeded. Outside interference would upset the smooth operation of the 'invisible hand'. This might include intervention from governments or religious and moral sources (although Adam Smith himself, a deist, believed that 'natural law' or providence would ensure that selfishness was kept in check by moral sympathy and the desire for the good opinion of one's peers. Only in the twentieth century would economists argue that economics is a 'science', from which values must be excluded).

All that is needed is for manufacturers to meet the felt needs of consumers, who could in turn express their freedom of choice to select between products. Efficiency in trading would result because only manufacturers making goods that people choose to buy will survive in the marketplace.

The attraction of New Right economics is its utter realism. Whereas forms of socialism optimistically hope that man is innately selfless and will work for the good of society at large if only his circumstances are right, the New Right knows that people are basically selfish. It attempts to harness this truth in such a way as to improve the lot of society generally.

Thatcherism even has its own version of Christianity to back it up. On Sunday 22nd May 1988 Margaret Thatcher addressed the General Assembly of the Church of Scotland on politics and morality. In the address she outlined a Christian basis for her economic policies. It is interesting to note that all the key points she drew out are the points at which the Bible seems to support the consumerist world-view.

When she said, 'Christianity is about spiritual redemption, not social reform', she was reinforcing the view that religious faith is primarily a personal matter, with little or no impact on the social sphere. She quoted St Paul, 'If a man will not work, he shall not eat'. Again the stress is on the individual, pursuing his or her own self-interest. One of the biblical passages most often quoted by the Prime Minister is that of the good Samaritan. But in Thatcher theology the message of the parable is not one of selfless caring, but that the Samaritan could not have helped the hurt man unless he had pursued his own self-interest by creating money to pay for room in the inn. And another of her famous statements is that there is no such thing as 'society', simply individuals and their families. It is a theology of consumerism.

Problems of the New Right

In one way the New Right is on target in that it recognises the truth about human nature. But this in turn gives rise to a range of other problems:

▷ If the system is built on the basis of self-interest, then everybody must be motivated by self-interest for it to work. In the words of Donald Hay, economics tutor at Jesus College, Oxford:

> If firms and households *fail* to press their own objectives, then the argument for the efficiency of capitalism falls.... It is no exaggeration to say that capitalism accepts human selfishness in the use of resources, and gives it respectability.[8]

▷ The stress on realism can lead to a squeezing out of any idealism. Even morality can be seen as a luxury to be tacked on when economic 'realities' have been dealt with. This has been particularly true of the new generation of younger Conservatives, many brought up without the same restraining hand of Christian-based morality of their parents' day. The only questions coming from Young Conservatives at a recent annual party conference I attended concerned efficiency, growth, success and personal freedom of choice. Moral checks were elbowed out as being 'unrealistic'. It was frightening to see a world-view at work which appeared to have avarice as its sole motivation.

The brutal realism of the consumer world-view has to be held in check by a higher moral law. Otherwise it becomes dangerous. It is true that theologians at the time of the

Reformation have been held responsible by historians for creating the conditions in which capitalism could flourish. And it is true that it was Calvin who overturned the traditional ban on charging interest which the church had upheld beyond the Middle Ages. But in Calvin's day unfettered greed was held in check by a firm code of Christian ethics. Calvin's words on this matter are uncompromising: 'We are not our own... We are God's'; 'We are (God's) stewards, and are bound to give account of our stewardship... the only right mode of administration is that which is regulated by love.' (Institutes).

Wealth is neutral. It can be used in ways which enhance human life. But it is only a *means* and not an *end*. As King Midas discovered, wealth pursued for its own sake becomes destructive.

▷ The idea that you have to create wealth before you can give any away sounds convincing. But at best it is only a half-truth. It is equally the case that the more wealth you have the more you want for yourself. According to the Charities' Aid Foundation, the people in the UK who give least to charity are those in the affluent South-East.

▷ Freedom of choice is an inadequate basis for organising society. One person's freedom is often another's lack of freedom. My freedom to play loud records is my neighbour's loss of freedom to have a quiet afternoon. His freedom to pick flowers is my loss of freedom to enjoy a beautiful park. My freedom to shop on Sunday is a retailer or shopworker's loss of a day at home with the family. My freedom to have unlimited credit by removing all legal restrictions is somebody else's increased risk of falling into debt. My freedom to drive a car eventually results in the loss of somebody else's freedom to have unpolluted lakes and healthy forests.

Freedom to choose is meaningless without a higher moral framework. It simply becomes the privilege of 'haves' over 'have nots'.

▷ There aren't enough natural resources in the world for everybody to live like Westerners. Even if we assume the consumer starting-point that universal prosperity is the surest way to happiness, you run up against the fact that the world's resources are limited.

Socialism

Even Marxists and socialists share much of the consumer world-view. In fact, in some respects, some socialism is more materialistic than the New Right in that it believes that by getting material conditions right, mankind's true potential will flourish. It shares the assumption that greater prosperity is the solution to our problems, but simply tells a different section of the community how to achieve it. As workers pursue their own self-interest (in the battle against the greedy employers) they will improve their own lot in life.

It has also been ironic to hear women of the left use rhetoric of the consumerist world-view in the issue of abortion. They call for 'a woman's right to choose', not questioning the assumption that self-interest is the ultimate court of appeal, even when it means killing. And a phrase currently popular in the USA is 'a woman's reproductive freedom', as if this kind of freedom could exist independent of consideration of her partner. A small group of left-wing feminists in the Labour Party, however, has given a more radical look at the issues at stake in abortion. They point out the irony that the only silent minority other left-wingers seem reluctant to speak out for is the unborn child. If self-interest is the final authority in the issue of abortion, why should it not be in the case of killing whales too? Or persecuting racial minorities?

I do not want to decry either left-wing aspirations towards a fairer society, or feminist claims that women have often been the victims of a male-dominated society and deserve more control over their own lives. I want to point out that many of their arguments are not radical enough. They share most of the assumptions of the unfair, male society they are rebelling against. At the end of the day they tend to have the same world-view as their enemies.

Morality

'Victorian Morality'

It is common these days to hear people speak disparagingly of 'Victorian morality', or 'old-fashioned' values. Why, people ask, should I be dictated to about what I can or can't do, particularly since the rules are based on the moral laws of a primitive culture from centuries ago? Mankind has grown up, thank you, and science has given us answers to the questions about life which people used to need faith or superstition to cope with. I want to run *my* life without outside restrictions and interference.

These are not just the views of your hairdresser, school teacher and milkman. They were the views which marked out a particular stage of European history which began in the eighteenth century, the Enlightenment.

The Enlightenment

Before the Enlightenment, morality in Europe was considered to have a firm, unshakeable basis: the word of God as revealed in the Bible. The Ten Commandments formed the core of everybody's understanding of right and wrong and the Old Testament Law formed the basis of most of the laws in European states.

The Enlightenment was an era of unparalleled scientific advances, the scientists and philosophers developed a faith that science and reason would give them answers to life's questions. The criteria of truth were 'Is it scientific?', 'Can it be proved?' Of course, when these tests were applied to God, the conclusion was 'No, there is no scientific proof for the existence of God.' In an age where the criterion of truth and knowledge was whether it could be seen or measured, religious faith no longer counted as 'truth'.

By the end of the eighteenth century many Enlightenment writers felt they had thrown off all traces of Christendom. One, the Marquis de Condorcet, wrote off the whole of the Middle Ages as an era of religious mumbo-jumbo:

> Man's only achievements were theological day-dreaming and superstitious imposture, his only morality religious intolerance... Europe awaited the moment when a new enlightenment would allow her to be reborn free, heiress to humanity and virtue.[9]

So a dualism developed: there were 'facts', which could be proved 'objectively' and there were 'values', which were subjective and beyond proof. The objective area included science, the subjective area religion and the system of morality which had accompanied it. Because the Enlightenment was an age when unprecedented trust was placed in science, this meant the 'objective' and provable was trusted more than the subjective and emotional. Faith and values were relegated to the intellectual dustbin of the Enlightenment and considered less worthy an object for study.

Aspects of the Enlightenment's Legacy

Our age has inherited the dualism begun in the eighteenth century. Only now many scientists and ordinary people do not believe that the areas of faith and values are necessary at all. The French biologist Jacques Monod writes in his classic book from the 1960s, *Chance and Necessity*:

> Chance *alone* is at the source of every innovation, of all creation in the biosphere. Pure chance, absolutely free but blind, at the very root of the stupendous edifice of evolution: this central concept of modern biology is no longer one among other possible or even conceivable hypotheses. It is today the *sole* conceivable hypothesis, the only one which squares with observed and tested fact.[10]

So, according to Monod and many other modern scientists, not only must you rigidly separate the two areas of facts and values, one is not needed. The sphere of facts is able to account fully for all the areas which used to be the sphere of faith: questions such as Who am I? Where am I going? Where did mankind come from? The logical consequence is that mankind is not *essentially* different from any other aspect of the material world. This was highlighted recently on the side of a bus advertising Edinburgh Zoo. It had a picture of a gorilla and bore the caption, 'Visit your relations this weekend.' Since Darwin, we find it hard to claim that mankind is in any real sense different from apes – a little more polite, and better at playing golf, perhaps, but not essentially different.

This is expressed concisely by the historian Jacob Bronowski: 'Man is a part of nature, in the same way that a stone is, or a cactus, or a camel.'[11]

This is the essence of materialism. The universe is a great machine, which runs by fixed laws that can be observed by science. The only thing that exists is the machine, the only thing that matters is the machine. Mankind too is a cog in the machine. Everything he does is conditioned by genes and environment. This attempt to reduce everything to scientific observation and exclude anything which doesn't fit is known as scientism – science elevated to the status of a religion. And at the heart of scientism is materialism – the belief that the only reality is matter and all that matters is matter.

Scientism was the perfect breeding-ground for the consumer world-view. Both share a stress on throwing overboard old-fashioned restrictions on personal freedom, and on the centrality of material, measurable things against fuzzy notions such as faith and morality. One says you can discover all there is to know by studying the material world, the other says you can experience all there is to enjoy in aspects of the material world.

Each, in its own way, assumes that the major rule of life is that newest is best. As we saw in Chapter 7, popularised evolutionary theory says the newest species to develop is superior to earlier species. Consumerism says the newest product must be best and that the old (no matter what its condition) can be thrown away as irrelevant. So, as I pointed out, the salesman, consumer and scientist (or at least, most scientific lay-people and *some* real scientists) share the same basic myth about life: newer is better. Older necessarily means inferior, old fashioned or 'unprogressive'.

But scientism has problems.

Problems with Scientism

The first problem for scientism is that it is based on false logic. The materialist says that the only things which are true and valid are those which can be scientifically proved or observed. But how can he prove that even his own statement is true? He cannot possibly know whether the things he can observe are all there is. Is he all-knowing, all seeing? All he can say is that he *believes* that only things which can be proved are true. But that means he is expressing a belief or faith, the very area he claims to have done away with! So materialism is self-contradictory from the start. The materialist makes a statement about truth and then can't even prove his own statement is true. He uses a statement of faith to claim that faith is not valid.

And when he claims mankind is 'progressing' he is making another statement of faith, one which goes against the evidence, but which he grimly clings onto as a creed. It is when a scientist goes beyond simple observation to make claims about values and ultimate truths that he becomes unscientific.

As such, the materialist's faith is no more provable or rational than, say, the Christianity the Enlightenment wanted to dump. How, then, do you decide which faith to accept? You have to decide which seems best to fit the facts. Most civilisations through history have found a religious answer more satisfactory than an irrational, one-dimensional materialism.

Under materialism, free will and rational thought become practically meaningless. Both of these imply that the thinker or doer can stand aside from a given situation to analyse it objectively. But, hang on! The materialist has said we're all cogs in the machine. How can we stand aside and look at the machine from a distance. Only the – ahem – maker of the machine can look at it with detachment. So the materialist is again inconsistent. He claims he can observe the natural world with objectivity, but at the same time says that he himself is just another part of that nature, pre-programmed by his genes and environment. How can he possibly know if he is seeing the whole picture, with true detachment, when he is not detached?

The whole of our legal system is based on the assumption that materialism is false. How could we punish a criminal if he had no genuine free will in his crime. If he was utterly 'programmed', he could hardly be blamed for his actions and it would be nonsense to punish him for something in which he had no choice.

Materialism goes against human experience. Love, creativity, faith, are all supposed to be mere chemical accidents, with no deeper significance. But, more seriously, the materialist has no basis for morals. Science can only observe 'things', so how can we derive values? As philosophers ask, how can we derive an 'ought' from an 'is'? It is not possible. And yet we live as if there are moral values which bind us. The English poet Coleridge pointed out the silliness of denying that good and evil exist, just because you can't see or touch them:

> Are not the experimentalists credulous even to madness in believing any absurdity, rather than believing the grandest truths, if they have not the testimony of their own senses in their favour?

When science cuts off moral considerations and ceases to be guided by them it becomes capable of any horror. This is described by C.S. Lewis as 'the evil reality of lawless applied science'. If morality is irrelevant, why not experiment on animals – or even humans, as the Nazis did? Why not rape the natural world's resources? Or force people to work in unhealthy, degrading conditions, or reduce women to sex objects? Why not experiment with mixing the foetuses of humans and apes to produce a race of sub-humans? This has already been suggested as a serious possibility by at least one eminent scientist.

We live in a world where we know that murdering an old lady, child abuse, experimentation on live humans, are evil. We have to have moral guidelines to live. Science needs to be directed by moral guidelines. If we do not get these from the knowledge that there is a universal, solid morality which applies to everybody (the values of the tree house outlined in my Introduction, upheld by the Judaeo-Christian tradition) then where can they come from?

Pick'n'Mix Morality

Many people in the modern world, despairing of any objective basis for morality, fall back on personal choice, a pick'n'mix morality which involves selecting the aspects of traditional morality which suit them best and ignoring the rest. This view is expressed not only by several scientists, but also by theologians, such as Don Cupitt:

> The changeover from religion as a set of objectively provided and unchangeable supernatural realities and values, to religion as a creative human activity by which new meanings and values are continually generated is certainly not easy. But we can do it, and we can learn to be rational about it.[13]

The consequences of the pick'n'mix morality are visible in our streets and homes. As long as the ideas sit with academics in ivory towers, all very well. But when they hit the street there is trouble. The football hooligan decides that his quest for 'continually generating new meanings and values' means knifing a fan of the opposing team. Or a gang may decide it means terrorising a local Asian family because they don't like the colour of their skin. The city yuppie decides it means naked self-interest, which treads on everybody else on the way to the top. And why not? If it is up to us to create our own values, who are you to criticise the values I choose for myself? The only basis you could possibly have for criticising the morality I choose by is by referring to a universal moral law which is binding on everybody of every religion and race (described by C.S. Lewis in *The Abolition of Man* as the *Tao*). It is only by agreeing to the rules of Monopoly that we can say somebody is wrong when they break those rules. But this is rejected by most modern Westerners. They say each person should be free to improvise their own rules.

The other consequence of privatised morality is that nobody feels that areas beyond the private are their concern. The city is a no-man's land which nobody really cares for. The world inside the front door may be neat, ordered, cared-for. Beyond the door is somebody else's responsibility, not mine. This helps explain the carefree way people fling rubbish into country lanes and city streets and the unloved, unloving atmosphere of our urban wastelands. Nobody feels the public arena is theirs in the way the private world of the home is theirs. And this attitude affects our view of discipline. I wouldn't dream of smacking somebody else's children if I saw them being naughty or hurting somebody. My neighbour's well-being is not my business. Wider social evils continue unchecked.

Iron-fist morality

The alternative to everybody picking their own morality is for one person, or a small group of people, to pick a morality for everybody else. Values and ethics and 'people's best interests' are dictated from a central power, which will not tolerate any deviation from the rules it has laid down.

This was seen in Hitler's Germany, Pol Pot's Cambodia, Stalin's Russia, Amin's Uganda, and can be seen in any number of dictatorships around the world today. Freedom of conscience is crushed and submitted to the 'morality' dictated by leaders. Hitler's morality was that Jews were an evil which had to be purged. Stalin's morality was that good equalled obedience to the state and evil was disobedience; no higher morality was allowed as a yardstick for measuring Stalinism. And Pol Pot's morality stated that intellectuals and artists were parasites who had to be eliminated. In every case one aspect of the universal morality upheld by Christianity is singled out (the value of the nation, the racial group, equality, science, progress) and all others rejected. It is a kind of pick'n'mix morality extended beyond the individual to the state as a whole.

More recently, several scientists in the 1960s seriously suggested that the way to universal happiness would be to put drugs in the water system, to keep everybody permanently ecstatic. But this too would mean dictatorship. Aside from the fact that most people would not want it and would be forced into it against their will, somebody would have to administer the drugs. Again, it means dictatorship – one person has the iron fist of power and others simply obey.

A young generation of Nazis, Cambodians, Russians, Ugandans were raised in a climate of warped moral values. But what right have we to say the morals are warped? Unless we have an objective, solid yardstick for measuring morality, how can we ever escape from the tyranny of pick'n'mix or iron-fist morality?

Most countries in the West still carry the roots of their traditional 'objective' morality, although many are rapidly trying to dig them up. But when roots are dug out you have to start again by planting new ones (after a revolution, coup or other violent change). If you deny a universal basis for values, relativism or totalitarianism are the only options, both of them paths which involve singling out bits of traditional morality and ignoring others.

Letters to Newspapers

Every few weeks somebody writes to their local newspaper with a letter something like the following:

> Dear Sir,
> I am writing to complain about the space you give local clergy to air their bigoted opinions. Don't you understand that religion has caused countless wars through history and untold bloodshed? The sooner humankind throws off the nonsensical superstitions of the past, the sooner we can build a better world without intolerance and gullibility.
> Yours sincerely.

I have read dozens of such letters down the years. And they are all equally wrong. History in fact proves the exact opposite: that when a country throws off its Christian heritage and its accompanying assertion of a solid basis for morality, any abomination can result. One of the French Enlightenment philosophers, Diderot, wrote of his longing 'to strangle the last king with the guts of the last priest'.[14] Not surprisingly, the French Revolution was followed by the blood-bath of the Reign of Terror, Hitler was able to gas six million Jews in the name of progress and enlightenment, Stalin removed 12 million of his opponents (according to the Soviet historian Roy Mevedev, the USSR's leading authority on the Stalin era;[15] Western estimates put the figure closer to 20 million). When I interviewed Bishop Festo Kivengere of Uganda he told me of roads lined with hundreds of thousands of skulls of the dead, both from Amin and the regime which followed.

The entire Spanish Inquisition only killed as many people as a few days in Hitler's gas chambers. Even the 'religious' troubles in Northern Ireland only see a fraction as many deaths annually as gang warfare in Los Angeles.

So let's have no nonsense about the world being better off without religion. The view of man as being in the image of God, with dignity and a firm, comprehensive set of moral values, is our only protection against what the historian Toyn-bee described as 'a sinister ancient religion' of 'the fanatical worship of collective human power'. He said the French Revolution was 'only the first of the mass-crimes that have been committed during the last hundred and seventy years in this evil religion's name'.[16]

When you dump Christianity, faith and values aren't dumped with it. They simply find another, less worthy, object. And this will demand obedience and, in many cases, human sacrifice.

The Modern Dilemma

When our children look for identity we point them towards a new pair of jeans or a trip to the cinema. When they yearn for heroism we give them sunglasses.

When people want to be valued as three-dimensional beings with meaning and purpose, we reduce them to one-dimensional pleasure machines. If I find my identity in mate-rial goods I am only as valuable as those goods. Whole areas of life are shut down because they don't fit. Self-esteem and relationships become precariously dependent on playing the game of achievement and prosperity.

When people yearn for satisfaction we tell them to find it in a bank-balance or shopping centre. But all human experience backs up the old Muslim quotation: 'Who so craves wealth is like a man who drinks seawater. The more he drinks the more he increases his thirst.' You are never satisfied, no matter how much you accumulate. We never feel we can relax and say 'enough is enough'.

The modern dilemma is that following the consumer world-view leads to alienation: between ourselves and others, our-selves and the planet, ourselves and satisfaction, ourselves and deeper values, and – ultimately – from ourselves. But the route which promises identity, meaning and a solid basis for values is dismissed as 'unscientific' or 'old fashioned'.

Back to Basics

Yet a world-view is about faith. As we have seen, no world-view can claim to be 'provable'. Even scientific materialism is based on an unprovable guess, contradicted by most human experience, that everything can be reduced to mechanical or chemical processes. So how can we choose a world-view? The answer ought to be to choose the one which best answers the human situation as we know it. But we don't choose in this way.

We 'catch' consumerism from our environment, like 'flu, and take it for granted that it has all the answers. And if we do ever question it we use a *consumer* assumption to judge the alternatives by – does it feel good to me, will it bring me happiness and prosperity?

If we rustle through the Enlightenment's dustbins we uncover an interesting fact: they threw out their Judaeo-Christian heritage not because it was proved untrue or because it did not fit the facts, but because of an emotionally based desire to be free of the past, to be free of the limitations tradition seemed to impose. And we have inherited these beliefs. G K Chesterton is right: in our day Christianity has not been tried and found wanting, it has been left untried.

Becoming Subversive

In a society which gives unthinking service to the consumer worldview Christian conversion is the most subversive act possible. It involves a radical shift of worldview, a denial of the most basic creeds of consumerism. It is not just the tickling of a severed, 'sacred' bit of a life, but an upheaval of one's attitude to values, relationships, possessions and identity.

Conversion is not giving mental assent to a set of ideas, it is entering a relationship. It affirms that relationship is at the heart of all that is real: relationship with the Creator and with other people. Christ's summary of the Old Testament law was to love God and love others and then tack yourself on as an afterthought (Mt 22:37–40). The doctrine of the Trinity tells us that relationship already existed in the very character of God before you and I were a twinkle in his eye. A relationship of love existed even before the universe began.

In the view from the tree-house with which I began this book, consumerism is recognised as a modern idolatry. In any age, idol worship means the elevation of an aspect of the created world to the status of a god. The Christian task in any age includes the dethroning of those cultural idols which take the place of the Creator. In themselves these things may be quite worthy (money, sex, nature, human reason, physical beauty, and any number of others). But idolatry selects one such dimension and sets it above the rest, making it a focus of meaning and significance.

The main idolatry of the modern West is consumerism, an unbalanced and unhealthy, self-centred obsession with money and the pleasures it can provide. Wealth becomes the goal of aspiration, the root of identity, the source of satisfaction. Little wonder that Christ personified mammon not simply as a greedy waywardness, but as a living and dangerous rival for the worship and adoration due to God.

The consumer idolatry sets up mammon as lord and gives its all in the worship of its god. It selects those aspects of the morality of earlier belief systems it likes and shuts down all the rest. It is modern mankind gaining the world and losing its soul.

The mind-blowing paradox of the tree-house, the upside-down Kingdom, is that only in reversing the consumer world-view and 'losing' ourselves can we actually find our true identity. It tells us that only by dethroning the cutlural idols of cash and consumption (which demand our servitude) can we find authentic freedom, and that, as we look for God and for others we actually begin to find ourselves.

But maybe that is not so strange a concept. Our own lives tell us that it is in those moments that we go beyond our own self-absorption that we feel truly human: falling in love; losing oneself in a good book or film, looking at an amazing painting or hearing beautiful music; going out of one's way to help somebody you normally wouldn't bother with; the time when as a teenager you had a religious experience which you now dismiss as 'an adolescent phase'.

The only way to transcend self-absorption is to acknowledge the reality of something (or somebody) beyond yourself which (or who) has a claim on you. The only way to learn is to submit your mind to a truth beyond itself.

Being Subversive

The word 'radical' means getting to the very roots of an issue. True radicalism is not calling for increased personal freedom and the overthrow of governments or old-fashioned morality; or saying the answer to the world's problems is getting material conditions right.

The radical is the person who begins to plant new roots, who challenges the very world-view of consumerism and affirms that *relationship* is the base on which the universe itself rests, that identity has a source beyond the shopping mall, and that morality is solid and objective. Radicalism is shouting with John the Baptist that an axe is laid to the rotting roots of our very culture (Lk 3:9). The true radical is Bishop Janani Luwum of Uganda, confronting Idi Amin and meeting an inevitable death; Martin Luther King, who so believed in human dignity that he was prepared to pay the cost of his own life; Mother Teresa of Calcutta, whose simple and selfless devotion is admired but is basically incomprehensible to the modern Western mind; Bishop Oscar Romero of San Salvador, gunned down in his cathedral while preaching on justice.

The radical is the old lady from the back row of the church who looks after her very elderly mother, gives herself to the service of others, prays nightly to a God who gives her strength and identity, and chuckles at the ludicrous idea that money can buy happiness.

Notes

1 EF Schumacher, *Small is Beautiful* (Abacus: London, 1974), p 228.
2 Andrew Brandon, *Health and Wealth* (Kingsway: Eastbourne, 1987), p 11.
3 Brandon, *op cit*, p 11.
4 Mike Yaconnelli, 'Becoming Pagan', *The Wittenburg Door* Nos 98 & 99 (August–November, 1987) p 64.
5 Steve Taylor, 'Who Ya Trying to Kid, Kid?', *I Want to be a Clone* (Word Records: London, 1984)
6 GK Chesterton, *Orthodoxy* (Bodley Head: London, 1908): p 122.
7 CS Lewis, *Miracles* (Fontana: London, 1960), p 98.
8 Donald Hay, *A Christian Critique of Capitalism* (Grove books: Nottingham, 1975), p 15.
9 Antoine-Nicolas de Condorcet, *Sketch for a Historical Picture of the Progress of the Human Mind* (1795), trans. June Barraclough (London, 1955) p 72.
10 Jacques Monod, *Chance and Necessity* (Collins: London, 1972)
11 Jacob Bronowski, *The Identity of Man* (Natural History Press: Garden City, 1965), p 2.
12 ST Coleridge, quoted by Basil Willey, *Samuel Taylor Coleridge* (WW Norton: New York, 1972).
13 Don Cupitt, 'A Generation to Improvise its Own Morality', *The Guardian* 31 October 1988 p 39.
14 Quoted in Bob Goudzwaard, *Capitalism and Progress* (Eerdmans: Grand Rapids, 1979) p 51.

[15] Rupert Cornwell, 'Russian historian says Stalin killed at least 12 million', *The Independent* 24 November 1988 p 14.

[16] Arnold Toynbee, Introduction, *The Gods of Revolution* by Christopher Dawson (New York University Press: New York, 1972): p x.

FOR FURTHER READING

Clark, Eric. *The Want Makers*. Hodder & Stoughton: London, 1988.

Elkington, John and Hailes, Julia. *The Green Consumer Guide*. Gollancz: London, 1988.

Guinness, Os. *The Gravedigger File*. Hodder & Stoughton: London, 1983.

Hartropp, Andrew (ed). *Families in Debt*. Jubilee Centre Publications: Cambridge, 1988.

Kraybill, Donald. *The Upside-Down Kingdom*. Marshall Morgan & Scott: Basingstoke, 1985.

Lewis, C S *The Abolition of Man*. Fount: Glasgow, 1978.

North, Richard. *The Real Cost*. Chatto & Windus: London, 1986.

Packard, Vance. *The Hidden Persuaders*. Penguin: London, 1957.

Packard, Vance. *The Waste Makers*. Penguin: London, 1960.

Porritt, Jonathon. *Seeing Green*. Basil Blackwell: Oxford, 1984.

Schluter, Michael. *Keeping Sunday Special*. Marshall

Pickering: Basingstoke, 1988.

Schumacher, E F *Small is Beautiful*. Abacus: London, 1974.

Sider, Ronald. *Rich Christians in an Age of Hunger*. Hodder & Stoughton: London, 1978.

Sine, Tom. *The Mustard Seed Conspiracy*. Marc Europe: London, 1981.

Storkey, Alan. *A Christian Social Perspective*. IVP: Leicester, 1979.

Taylor, John. *Enough is Enough*. SCM: London, 1975.

Taylor, Peter. *The Smoke Ring*. Sphere: London, 1985.

Walter, Tony. *All You Love is Need*. SPCK: London, 1985.

KEY ORGANISATIONS

Christian Ecology Group
58 Quest Hills Rd
Malvern
Worcestershire
WR14 1RW

Familybase Freedom From Debt Campaign
Jubilee House
3 Hooper St
Cambridge
CB1 2NZ

Friends of the Earth
377 City Rd
London
EC1V 1NA

Intermediate Technology Development Group
Myson House
Railway Terrace
Rugby
CV21 3BR

Keep Sunday Special Campaign
Jubilee House
3 Hooper St
Cambridge
CB1 2NZ

New Consumer
52 Elswick Rd
Newcastle upon Tyne
NE4 6JH

Open Christian College
83 Brampton Rd
Cambridge
CB1 3HJ

Traidcraft plc
Kingsway
Gateshead
NE11 0NE

The Lost And The Dreamer

by Naomi Starkey

Earth was diseased, burnt out. Two colony ships escaped. One was lost...

The settlement that grows from the surviving ship is in despair and disarray: families and civilisation break down as the colonists, repeating the mistakes of their forebears, ravage the new world of Osiris and fell the forests.

Four wanderers flee the riots and looting, their hearts fired with the dream of a better world. While Anno struggles on, impatient for freedom, Minna turns to dreams of a Prince with golden eyes who will come to her rescue. As they struggle over the pitiless mountains, facing betrayal and bloodshed, few signs of hope remain. Is there truly a Prince? Will he come?

'Enjoyable reading—a vivid tapestry.'

—**Fay Sampson**

Minstrel
Monarch Publications